PRESSURE

FROM FBI FUGITIVE TO FREEDOM

MALIK WADE

FOREWORD BY JEFF ADACHI
SAN FRANCISCO PUBLIC DEFENDER

PRESSURE PUBLISHING

SAN FRANCISCO

Published by:
Pressure Publishing
3801 3rd St., #1004
San Francisco, CA 94124
www.malikwade.info

Ordering Information: To order this book, please visit our website or write to the publisher at the address above, or email the author at malikwade415@gmail.com.

Copyright © 2017 by Malik Wade

All rights reserved. This book or any portion thereof may not be reproduced, displayed, or used in any manner whatsoever without the express written permission of the publisher except for the use of brief quotations in a book review.

Project Manager: Marla Markman, www.marlamarkman.com
Developmental Editor: Dana Fitchet
Copy Editor: Tammy Ditmore, www.editmore.com
Cover and Interior Design: GKS Creative, www.gkscreative.com
Cover Photo: JD Harris
Back Cover Photo: Jayvon "Hitz"

Publisher's Cataloging-in-Publication Data
Names: Wade, Malik, author.
Title: Pressure : from FBI fugitive to freedom / Malik Wade.
Description: Includes index | San Francisco, CA: Pressure Publishing, 2017.
Identifiers: ISBN 978-0-9986167-0-4 (pbk) | 978-0-9986167-1-1 (ebook) | LCCN 2016918554
Subjects: LCSH Wade, Malik. | Drug dealers--United States--Biography. | Inner cities—United States. | Urban youth. | African American men--Social conditions. | Imprisonment--United States. | Prisoners--United States--Biography. | Corrections--United States. | BISAC BIOGRAPHY & AUTOBIOGRAPHY / Personal Memoirs
Classification: LCC HV5805 .W33 2017 | DDC 363.45092--dc23

LCCN: 2016918554

978-0-9986167-0-4 (Softcover)
978-0-9986167-1-1 (eReaders)

Printed in the United States of America

23 22 21 20 19 18 17 / 11 10 9 8 7 6 5 4 3 2 1

To my grandmother, Gladys Starks, the mighty matriarch of my family, who had 16 children, 68 grandchildren, 110 great-grandchildren, and 18 great-great-grandchildren, Granny, you are irreplaceable.

CONTENTS

FOREWORD BY JEFF ADACHI,
   SAN FRANCISCO PUBLIC DEFENDER ix
INTRODUCTION
   THE HERO'S JOURNEY 1
   MY SAN FRANCISCO 5

PART I: THE PATH TO DESTRUCTION
   Chapter 1 HOW IT ALL BEGAN 11
   Chapter 2 SEDUCTION 17
   Chapter 3 FALSE VICTORY 19
   Chapter 4 A FATHER'S IMPACT 27
   Chapter 5 HUBRIS 33
   Chapter 6 TROUBLE IN PITTSBURGH 37
   Chapter 7 THE CHASE IS ON 45
   Chapter 8 THE PHONE CALL 53
   Chapter 9 THE FUGITIVE 59
   Chapter 10 THE POWER OF CONDITIONING 67
   Chapter 11 INSATIABLE AND UNTOUCHABLE 73
   Chapter 12 ART OF THE DEAL 81
   Chapter 13 FACE THE MUSIC 89
   Chapter 14 TRANSFER 99
   Chapter 15 FINDING MY WAY 105
   Chapter 16 MENTAL WARFARE 111

Chapter 17 TRUE EDUCATION 119
Chapter 18 LET THE GAMES BEGIN 125
Chapter 19 PRESSURE MANIFESTED 129
Chapter 20 RELIGION VS. SPIRITUALITY 137
Chapter 21 MASTER STUDENT 143

PART II: RETURNING, RELEARNING, RESTORING

Chapter 22 A NEW WORLD 153
Chapter 23 STAYING FOCUSED 163
Chapter 24 PRISON'S IMPACT ON
RELATIONSHIPS AND SELF 171
Chapter 25 BERKELEY 177
Chapter 26 MENTORSHIP 185
Chapter 27 STREETS TO STANFORD 197
Chapter 28 THE JOURNEY 207
Chapter 29 THE RIDDLES OF THE WORLD 215
Chapter 30 THE BIRTH OF SOMETHING BEAUTIFUL 225
Chapter 31 COLLEGE BOUND 235
Chapter 32 I CAN BREATHE 241
Chapter 33 THE POWER OF LISTENING 249
Chapter 34 AN OPEN LETTER TO MY COMMUNITY 257

ACKNOWLEDGMENTS 267

DON'T BE AFRAID TO SHARE
YOUR STORY. IT MIGHT INSPIRE OTHERS.

—*Malik Wade*

FOREWORD

There is no better than adversity. Every defeat, every heartbreak, every loss, contains its own seed, its own lesson on how to improve your performance the next time.
—Malcolm X

You may think you know this story. A man lives the high life of a drug dealer, becomes a fugitive, goes to prison for a long time, and eventually redeems himself. But you would be wrong. Malik Wade's story is much, much more. While *Pressure* is a story about a man existing in Dante's Inferno who transformed himself into an educated and enlightened person, it will also take you on Malik's sometimes painful but never boring journey that has led him to who he is today: the educator, thought-provoker, and change-maker, who is challenging us as a society and people to think differently and radically. And at a time when our planet needs leaders like him most.

You probably have read the statistics: One out of three Black men will have a criminal conviction in his lifetime. There are more Black men in prison in the United States than the total collective prison populations of ten large countries, including India, Japan, Canada, Germany, and England. Five times as many Whites are using drugs as Blacks, yet Blacks are sent to prison for drugs at 10 times the rate of Whites. Even in Malik's progressive hometown of San Francisco, 56 percent of the people arrested are Black, while our Black population is less than 5 percent. And with 70 percent of those released from prison and jail returning to cages within a year, we know the system is failing us. But the statistics don't tell the complete story of what is really happening and why. That's where Malik comes in.

Pressure is also a story about survival, winning and losing, heartbreak, hopelessness, and how the light at the end of the tunnel finally appears for those whose faith is tested. This story benefits from the pace and feel of an action-packed Hollywood movie, but it contains important lessons for executives, politicians, organizers, and anyone in a position of leadership. Although it can serve as a primer for those seeking a better understanding of social justice, Malik's story is written in a way that speaks directly to inner city youth and others victimized by poverty, over-criminalization, and inadequate education. They, too, need to read this book and apply its lessons.

Malik's metamorphosis from street-tough thug to accomplished leader belies the fact that he never wavered from his authentic self. He simply chose to apply himself differently. Like Malcolm X, he began reading voraciously in prison, and like Mandela or Gandhi, he used his enlightenment for good. He did so by re-examining his core beliefs and redefining his priorities and goals in life. Instead of selling a brick of cocaine, he learned how to mine the ideas that would give rise to a successful education. Instead of running from the law, he found his footing in teaching others to avoid trouble and enjoy the stability and security of a life well lived. Instead of disappearing into his success, he is using it to help others who would benefit from his life experience, mistakes, and triumphs.

Malik's story gives us a glimpse into the potential our society could unlock if it freed the countless souls it has incarcerated, forgotten, and written off. Imagine the talent we have already lost by locking away an entire generation of black and brown men, women, and children.

The damage wrought by decades of mass incarceration has only recently begun to recede. During his eight years in office, President Barack Obama commuted 1,927 sentences, more than any president since President Harry S. Truman. In his final week, he granted 273 clemency petitions, including many who sought to reduce their sentences under an initiative to shorten prison terms for nonviolent federal inmates convicted of drug crimes. But there are still 2.3 million people in prisons and jails, most for drug-related crimes. Nearly half of them are black. How many of them were equally deserving of clemency or at least a reduction in their sentences?

As the elected Public Defender for the City of San Francisco, and a criminal defense attorney for over 30 years, I have witnessed firsthand the cruelty, pain, and suffering of a criminal injustice system that is out of control. Life sentences for minors, a three-strikes law that still puts people away for several lifetimes for nonviolent crimes, and a bail system that keeps the poor behind bars while the rich buy their freedom.

My office, fortunately, is funded at an appropriate level and we are able to provide clients with the best legal representation money can't buy. We have the social workers, paralegals, investigators, educational advocates, and support staff to help people turn their lives around. We even employ six community organizers who work with youth and families in those neighborhoods most affected by poverty and lack of opportunity. But many public defender offices around the country lack the resources so freely given to law enforcement, and as a result, are unable to provide the type of legal representation our Constitution requires. Malik's story warns that if we do not invest in our children on the front end, we will surely pay a terrible price at the back end. As Frederick Douglass wrote, "It is easier to build strong children than to repair broken men (and women)."

One cannot ignore the fact that our country's movement toward criminal justice reform has taken a big step backward given the current administration's stance on bail reform, mass incarceration, and monitoring of police departments by the federal government. But it is being met with fierce resistance. Black Lives Matter and the movement for reforming our police and court system are stronger than ever. People have been shaken from their complacency and given a pressing reason to fight for fairness, equality, and diversity.

To begin to heal the damage of racism and mass incarceration, we must understand the severity of the wounds. Tucked deep into Malik Wade's story you will find the seeds from which new life and hope can spring. His salvation is our salvation. His triumph against all odds is a testament to what is possible if we help, rather than hinder, the former incarcerated in our communities.

Jeff Adachi
San Francisco Public Defender

INTRODUCTION
THE HERO'S JOURNEY

No one is perfect in this imperfect world.
—*Patrice Lumumba*

My world suddenly stopped. I couldn't feel my limbs. Things moved in slow motion as I stood blankly staring at the judge who had just sentenced me to 169 months in federal prison. The previous twenty-nine years of my life flashed before my eyes. The kickball games on the elementary school playground, algebra tests in high school, my first kiss. And so much more.

Pressure chronicles my passage through the world—describing the evolutionary stages of a boy misguidedly meandering about on the path to become a man and how he is ultimately redeemed and "made whole." The book tracks my transformation from inquisitive little boy and student athlete to community advocate, mentor, Stanford Law School and UC Berkeley guest lecturer, and executive director of my own nonprofit organization, the Scholastic Interest Group. But that transformation also includes a career as a nationwide drug dealer, a place on the FBI's wanted list for seven years, and an inmate in federal prison for more than twelve.

The pieces of the story provide deep insight into my psyche at various stages of my transformation. The growth and development brought by each stage played huge roles in making up and bringing together the ingredients of who I am today.

This memoir is made up of many different stories that compose the larger narrative and are part and parcel of a much greater truth. I am just a microcosm, but a small sample of society. However, while my story is specific to my life as a Black male from the city, it also transcends race, gender, and culture as well as philosophical and intellectual bents and schools of thought. There are many common denominators. *Pressure* covers a lot of ground and will resonate with many demographics: "at-risk" youth, single parents, corporate executives, college professors, the sociologically curious, and—of course—those in downtrodden and underprivileged communities throughout the world. Actually, this book will be appreciated by anyone who has faced "a dark night of the soul."

My story is a human story. It touches on the human element that connects us all and is a vivid account of the infinite possibilities both negative and positive. I invite you to allow it to reach your deepest emotions and pinch your spirit. Allow your senses to be stimulated and your mind opened as you inject yourself into certain scenes and situations.

My hope is that many moments throughout the book will move you to ask, "Have I ever experienced a similar emotion? Have there been instances in my life that relate to his story?" A scene may remind you of a parallel situation or a moment with your spouse or children, or a description may trigger a memory of a schoolteacher, professor, business partner, or friend. Human moments are universal.

In this account, I offer my counter narrative to many of the common conceptions that some people have about drug dealers, people who go to prison, and people who grow up in the inner city or in communities under fire. Many think that anyone who fits these descriptions is less than human, that we're desensitized robots without compassion or emotions, functioning as primal animals, lacking basic intelligence, and acting out indiscriminately. This is unquestionably not true. We all cry. We all hurt. We all feel. We all think. No group has a monopoly on emotions or human feelings.

I have lectured at several universities and spoken about many of these misperceptions, which have often been made popular by sociologists, criminal justice professors, and other supposedly objective onlookers who arrive at their sometimes flawed and limited conclusions by allowing data and statistics to take precedence over empirical experience. *Pressure* is an integration of the two, wedding objective hard data with practical experience.

The narrative that follows is 100 percent factual to the best of my recollection. I haven't changed names or reconstructed any scene or moment. There is no need for aliases because the book's focus is on me, and any incrimination is self-inflicted. This memoir is my truth.

Along my journey, I met two pivotal people during my "rites of passage" that I must mention here.

When I was a young boy, I met a man named James Hodges. James was a local community activist and private investigator in San Francisco, my hometown. He was a big, strong man well over six feet tall—powerfully built, masculine, and smart. I respected his strength and level of consciousness, but what I liked most was the big beautiful smile on his face whenever he saw me. Every time we met, James would give me inspiring words of encouragement, telling me that I was strong and smart and that he believed in me. My young Black male ears needed to hear such words, and they left a permanent imprint on me.

The second pivotal person was Ms. Mooney, my third-grade teacher at Bayshore Elementary School. She was an exceptionally overweight White lady with a grumpy attitude who almost crushed my confidence as a child. One day she said, "Malik, you are never going to be anything." At many periods in my life, it might have seemed that Ms. Mooney was a prophet who could see into a crystal ball. But her words ultimately became as empowering to me as spinach is to Popeye. Today, I use them as a source of motivation when I speak at Stanford Law School and UC Berkeley, when I teach a class at Juvenile Hall, or when I mentor youth through my nonprofit organization. By trying to hurt me, Ms. Mooney ultimately helped me. As the Bible says, "What the devil meant for bad God uses for good" (Gen. 50:20).

Pressure was written for my supporters and detractors alike; perspectives from both sides are empowering.

I parallel my journey to a phenomenon called "the hero's journey," made popular by American scholar Joseph Campbell. "The hero's journey" starts, like any journey, with a typical story—in this case my childhood. As the journey continues, the hero experiences many trials and tribulations, including spiritual and mental transformation. The journey ends when the hero returns to help others with information learned along the way.

The pivotal point of my own hero's journey came on April 12, 2000, when special agents from the FBI arrested me in Minneapolis, Minnesota. As I told kids at the San Francisco Juvenile Justice Center in 2015, "From the moment the ice cold handcuffs hit my wrists, I knew that things had to change."

But there were many moments before that one when I did not want—or did not know how—to change things. I turn to those years of my journey first.

MY SAN FRANCISCO

San Francisco, my hometown, is a breathtakingly beautiful city. People flock from all over the world to see its legendary landmarks and magnificent tourist attractions. However, though seemingly safe on the surface, the streets of San Francisco have a sinister and seedy undercurrent—a low key but thriving criminal element that gets very little attention.

The media intentionally shies away from exposing San Francisco's dark and not so flattering side, including its history of discrimination against Blacks and the embarrassing fact that, largely due to gentrification, its Black population is only 3 percent in a city of nearly 837,000. To protect the city's multimillion-dollar tourism industry and its supposedly pristine liberal image, the media focuses on Oakland, a city just a few miles away, over the Bay Bridge. By some rankings, Oakland is among the top five most violent cities in America. This seems to suit San Franciscans and, more particularly, criminals in San Francisco—like my former self—just fine. It means less negative heat for all.

Police and law enforcement officials in San Francisco tend to use less aggressive policing tactics than their colleagues in other major metropolitan cities in the United States, contributing to far fewer federal prosecutions and sweeping indictments in the city. So, for a major metropolitan city, San Francisco doesn't have a sensational or sexy crime reputation like New York, Los Angeles, or Chicago; juicy and scandalous headlines running across the bottom of the screen on national news networks rarely involve San Francisco. Neither does the city have a great deal of criminal clout. To my knowledge, there's never been an observable presence of the Italian or Russian Mafia, or any other easily recognizable criminal factions or high-powered gangs. Unlike in most major cities, crooks in San Francisco are typically independent operators, and they are less likely to join up and form large criminal networks. No Crips and Bloods, Gangster Disciples, or Vice Lords.

Because gangs weren't common in San Francisco when I was coming of age, my early criminal influences were not gang members but individual guys in my community who were hustlers—moneymen who made a lot of money plying the drug trade. We called them "ballers." They shrewdly operated and maneuvered the streets like CEOs of large corporations. They were known for their sophisticated street smarts, quick wits, and high-level business expertise. They were sharp—yet smooth—businessmen, usually disguised and under the radar, not flashy or flamboyant.

While not particularly violent, these men were still far from being pushovers; violence was the last resort and only exacted when totally necessary, but if and when it was, it was serious. And ended with a period. They prided themselves on having solid reputations as enterprising entrepreneurs and being the polar opposite of the average thug or petty dope dealer. I was tutored and trained under close watch and learned, among other things, that being too colorful was taboo—being too showy could cause you to be cold-shouldered by these hustlers.

They were blunt and straightforward in their directives and dictates to me: "Nobody wants or needs any additional heat from the Feds," they said. They moved and thought like the Mob: violence was bad for business. I took that philosophy and ran with it, and it would become my business model throughout my drug career. I operated as a calculating CEO and master politician while navigating the streets of San Francisco, Pittsburgh, Minneapolis, and anywhere else I set up shop.

Despite this solid foundation, I developed a method of operation that was risky and somewhat complicated. It had to be employed cleverly because some might read my low-key and humble attitude as a sign of weakness that could expose me to potential aggressors. However, I ultimately felt confident in my ability to outsmart the would-be sharks and always prepared back-up plans and secret strategies to negate potential threats.

Part of my strategy for "the opposition" was to intentionally be mysterious. I started off by deciding I wouldn't look the part of a drug dealer. I would look like a fresh-faced, clean-cut college student and athlete. I would drive an old, beat-up 1977 Datsun B-210, which allowed me to fly under the Feds' radar. Appearing outwardly humble allowed me to be underestimated by would-be adversaries. This ultimately gave me a distinct competitive advantage as my would-be enemies and vultures mistakenly misjudged me and took me lightly, allowing me to stun them into unsuspecting submission. To stay focused on my tactics, I would keep close a copy of Sun Tzu's *The Art of War*. At the time, it was my holy book.

I learned early to play for keeps. Selling drugs was a zero-sum game with clear winners and clear losers. It was a game of intellectual gamesmanship with touches of violence—a thinking man's game—and certainly not for the faint of heart. It required outwitting the Feds and the sharks and trying to beat the odds. It was a deadly game of Russian roulette.

PART 1

THE PATH TO DESTRUCTION

1
HOW IT ALL BEGAN

My drug-dealing career started at the age of fifteen when I was growing up in San Francisco in the 1980s. Back then, San Francisco was flooded with cocaine, and crack cocaine was the most popular drug being sold on the street. Growing up in low-income housing, the son of a single parent struggling to support three children, selling drugs seemed like a welcome opportunity at the time.

My decision was motivated by the desire to make money to support myself and my family; it was a strategic economic decision, one that was all too often made by young Black boys at that time. However, I would not be telling the entire truth if I claimed that my idea to sell drugs was not tinged—or at least subliminally influenced—by dreamy visions of material wealth beyond survival. A chance for, as Kanye West says, "living the good life."

At the time I wasn't mature or mentally developed enough to understand the far-reaching consequences of my decision to sell drugs. I couldn't possibly understand the impact that it could—and eventually would—have on my life, my family's life, and my community.

I started drug dealing— hustling, I called it—as a sophomore in high school. Although I participated in sports and played on the state championship high school basketball team at Jefferson High in Daly City, my off-the-court life was much different than those of my teammates. When school let out, I transformed from a student–athlete to a drug dealer. Instead of leaving school with biology books, I had a brick of cocaine and a 9-millimeter pistol in my backpack. My "norm" rapidly transformed from that of a typical high schooler to a far darker and less innocent reality.

In my first year of hustling, I left home one Saturday around 6:00 a. m. and rode my beach cruiser bike up the street to the Sunnydale housing projects. This was to be the first day of my career as a newly initiated dope dealer. I had a small sack of crack rocks in a Ziploc sandwich bag tied in a knot, concealed and tucked tightly against my nuts in my boxer briefs, just in case the police stopped and frisked me. As I got close to the projects, I could see there was no one outside. The closer I got, the slower I pedaled, and the more nervous I became. To shake my fear, I said to myself, "You can do it. Let's get this money."

Suddenly, out of nowhere, a beat-up looking car drove up. Inside the car was a White couple. My senses immediately went on red alert. *Booyow*! They must be dope fiends, I thought. The only White folks that came around that way were dope fiends or undercover police officers. The car drove directly to me. I anxiously walked over to the driver side of the car. There was a pregnant pause and thick tension in the air. It was like in the movies when you hear a dramatic drum roll in the background. The couple in the car looked raggedy and worn out, like they had been up for days. The driver rolled the window down as I pulled out my sack of rocks; I placed a couple of them in his hand.

"How much you spendin'?"

"Forty," the driver said.

Suddenly he whipped out a huge chrome .357 Magnum and aimed it at my chest. I panicked. Dropping the bike and the rocks in the middle of the street, I ran away as the car sped off.

After they burned off with a palm full of my dope without paying me, I stumbled back into the street on trembling legs to scoop up the rocks that had fallen and retrieve my beach cruiser.

Although it took me a few minutes to get my nerves back under control, I stayed out there on the block until I made my first sale. After a couple of hours, I went home to count the morning take. It was a few hundred bucks. Not bad. Better than working at a McDonald's, I figured.

I was young and naive; I didn't think about how those two dope fiends could have splashed my brain matter all over my bike. I focused only on the money that I could make. I was hooked after the first sale—hypnotized by the fast cash! From that day on, I pursued drug dealing as a full-time occupation.

Most drug dealers start out small. I was no exception; I had to start from the bottom. I did not start out dealing with cartel members with huge duffel bags full of coke. I had to start like the rest of my friends with $20 and "double up" to make $40 and so on. However, eventually, those hundreds of $20 crack sales and the nights I spent hustling allowed me to move up in the ranks and buy in bulk. That allowed me to benefit from what legitimate business calls "the economies of scale," which simply means that the more money I spent, the more drugs I could buy—and sell.

While I was still in high school, I was able to get connected with a cartel courier who would sell me all the cocaine I wanted. Every week I would go to "the store" and spend between $7,500 and $15,000 with him. The most pivotal moment came when I purchased my first brick of powder cocaine, which was worth $15,000 back then. This was a huge deal considering I was still in high school. In the game, the more bricks you bought, the more large quantities you sold, and the more prestige and respect you got. I did this for a couple of years until I was eventually ready to expand my business and climb the "corporate" ladder of the drug world.

As soon as I graduated from high school, I started to sell drugs nationwide, first in Washington, D.C., then New York, then Pittsburgh, Pennsylvania. At the time, I was nineteen, arrogant, and on cruise control. I was "working" at my leisure, sometimes making multiple $15,000 transactions daily between eating my favorite dish of filet mignon and jumbo shrimp scampi at Ruth's Chris Steakhouse or flying to Las Vegas to Caesars Palace casino to sit ringside at the Mike Tyson fights.

The money was great, but selling dope wasn't for the softhearted; it came with many deadly occupational hazards, like the Feds, hijackers and kidnappers, and the "Narcs," or the narcotics squad. The Feds and the Narcs were already hot on my heels and had previously raided and ransacked my mother's home, where they found a 9-mm pistol. They also had informants who told them my every move.

In addition, convicts and killers who had recently been released from San Quentin penitentiary often moved back into the neighborhood and tried to extort and pressure the weak. I had to always stay on guard and "ready" for them. In the '80s, the streets started to get more violent as cash flowing from crack sales supplied more money for enemies to buy guns they could use against—well—*me*. If I wanted to survive, I had to stay sharp on all four corners.

Handling large sums of cash at an early age was stressful, as I couldn't trust anybody, and I had no place to hide my money. I knew that cash was king, but I was inexperienced about the financial system of banking and how credit worked. I didn't have a financial advisor or accountant to sit down with me to discuss stocks and bonds, how to invest my money, or how to purchase a house or piece of property, but I knew how to let my money pile up and not spend every cent as soon as I got it. I had a lot of cash, but no guidance or direction and couldn't invest it anyway because I had no job or any way to verify my income.

Because I was young and naive about the value of money, it would in the end evaporate like steam. A terrible habit I developed at the time was gambling away thousands of dollars in craps games on the street corner or in Las Vegas or Atlantic City, New Jersey. Little did I realize at the time that this habit would be part of the reason I would have nothing to show for the many days I ducked the Feds, dodged robberies, won shootouts, or survived kidnap attempts. I had no business franchises, no big house on the hill in the gated community—all I really retained were sleepless nights of paranoia and the Feds patiently waiting in the wings.

Although I thought I was naturally smart, in reality, I was a young, immature drug dealer who had very little experience in the world. My world was, in fact, very small, and my thinking was limited; I couldn't see things from a global, economic, or worldly perspective. I had little experience outside of the hood.

Early in my career I vowed to never use drugs, which in retrospect was a sinister contradiction. I made the decision to be a parasite and a predator by selling drugs, yet I knew enough to protect myself from their grip. It's an irony that I would have to deal with throughout my drug career.

2
SEDUCTION

The allure of drug dealing felt as sexy and tempting as being seduced by Beyoncé. Everything about it was overpowering to my senses, especially the money; I lusted for the smell of crisp, new $100 bills, and I loved money's erotic and sensuous nature. For me, selling drugs and making money was driven by an irresistible impulse.

Drug dealing was my first real crush. I willingly surrendered and gave my heart to it, and by the age of sixteen, the life of the streets and selling dope had a fierce and firm grip on me. While most high school kids set goals of going to college or getting a summer job, my ambitions included owning 100 Adidas sweat suits (with shoes to match) and keeping a steady drug connect.

The adrenaline rush of standing outside in the projects making hundreds—sometimes thousands—of dollars every day was far more attractive to me than going to school with a bunch of square kids and mainly White teachers who didn't understand me or my lifestyle. Even though I went to school and basketball practice every day, they both seemed a corny waste of time. I felt like I got straight As outside the classroom; selling crack required expertise in mathematics, economics, and social studies all at once. This was all I needed to be successful. Or so I thought.

Every time I made a drug sale, I felt like King Solomon sitting on his throne: untouchable and all-knowing. I thought I didn't have to listen to my teachers at school. Why would I? I made more money than they did. Right?

I also stopped listening to my basketball coach. Although he was a good man, to me he was—much like my teachers—a square White dude who didn't understand where I came from. What could he teach me? My arrogance and sense of superiority also impacted my relationships with my peers: I felt that I was better than my friends at school; I was wearing $200 Adidas sweat suits and they weren't. My mother? Well, she couldn't tell me very much those days either. Financially, I was taking care of myself now. I believed I was a grown-ass man.

My grand sense of cockiness and conceit cut me off from a rational sense of reality. One symptom of the disconnect was boldness; I didn't get nervous the way I should have when "riding dirty" and going to meet my drug connects. Riding with kilos of cocaine was a federal offense even for a juvenile, but the melodramatic nature of the drug game and the drama and suspense of it all made me feel like Scarface, or Nino Brown in the movie *New Jack City*. These films glorified the role, and I bought into it. I often rode in what we call a "bucket"—a car that typically costs $400 to $500. Yet I'd be riding with $50,000 in a school backpack on the back seat. The irony of it often made me nervously giggle rather than stop to consider the potential consequences of my decisions.

I got my first taste of the consequences one day when I was a budding sixteen-year-old drug dealer.

3
FALSE VICTORY

As the car slowly creeps by, I instinctively do a double take when I see four burly White boys inside the vehicle. Suspicious. Four White boys in the middle of the housing projects that are 90 percent Black has got to be a setup. They must be undercover cops. I smell trouble.

I accidentally make eye contact with the guys in the car. Damn, it's Red Beard and his crew. Red Beard was the meanest and most brutal police officer in the neighborhood. It was 1988, and the San Francisco streets were hot and getting more violent by the day. The police needed someone like Red Beard to keep the projects and young dope dealers in check. He was known to terrorize young brothers in the hood, typically harassing them on sight.

As we eyeball each other, my heart rate suddenly speeds up. I start to get jumpy as their car slows to a crawl. I think to myself, "Are your shoes laced tight?" Tight enough to get away if I need to, that is. As soon as the thought crosses my mind, all four car doors fly open, and the men burst out of the car with pistols pointed in my direction. I instantly take off running.

They split up and head in different directions in an attempt to trap me. I feel like a quarterback fleeing from a linebacker. In the background I hear them urgently radioing for additional backup. I think I hear a shot whistle by me. Damn! Now desperate, I run even faster, sprinting through the projects at full stride.

I have a 9-mm pistol and drugs on me and need to get some distance between the police and me so that I can dump them. Without breaking stride, I throw the weapon and drugs in some nearby bushes. I am clean now but can't stop running. Although I had not needed to run from the police often before this point, I had been taught by older guys around me to never stop—whether in the right or in the wrong. I subconsciously follow those lessons in this moment. If they catch me, they are sure to beat and bloody me. I feel like a fugitive slave being chased through the woods by bloodhounds and slave catchers.

My breathing gets heavy, and I start to gasp for air. But I am in excellent physical condition, super athletic and agile. My age works in my favor as I continue to run, although I'm winded. In addition, this is my stomping ground; I know all of the dead ends, vacant buildings, and good hiding spots. My knowledge of these projects joins forces with my youthful advantage and ensures that they can't catch me now.

After running for a couple of minutes—a very long time when running from the police—I peek from behind a building and see the police desperately driving in circles searching for me. I watch them from a distance as they finally call off the chase. They look frustrated and mad as hell. They finally quit the pursuit and drive out of the projects. Unsure of whether or not they're really leaving the area, I anxiously watch and wait a few minutes before I resurface from my hiding spot.

I immediately but cautiously go back to the bushes to recover my pistol and drugs. I can't find the gun, but I do find the drugs right where I had thrown them.

In the aftermath of this catastrophic circus, a small crowd has huddled up. As I walk back toward my car, they make me feel as if I am taking a victory lap. Several people in the crowd subtly and symbolically cheer me on, giving me thumbs up and looks of respect for getting away from the police.

In a challenged and economically depressed community such as the Sunnydale projects, any perceived victory against "the system" was welcomed, since we felt the system was responsible for our challenges in the first place. The community's visible support of my successful escape from the police was looking out for one of its own and giving the "fuck-you finger" to the system. It was our version of poetic justice.

At the time, I was ignorant to the downright dysfunction of fleeing from the police with a gun and drugs on me in the first place. And I didn't completely understand the puzzling paradox of a community that uncritically supported my criminality. In retrospect, their support came because a number of prior occasions had signified that the police were not on the side of the community. For instance, we had seen many unarmed young Black men who were not gang members or drug dealers gunned down for no apparent reason.

So in the collective mind of the community, although they did not know the circumstances of the chase, it was natural for them to cheer, "Run, Malik, run!" Lacking the sociological critique that I now possess, I welcomed the praise and symbolic cheers of the community at the time. I silently but smugly delighted in victory. Ultimately, though, it was a false victory—a victory that would have a detrimental cost in the long run. However, for a fleeting moment, I felt like a champion. It was irony of the highest order.

The situation could have ended disastrously. I could have been shot and killed. Adrenaline could have overpowered and paralyzed my thinking and made me unthinkingly "reach" for my pistol against my better judgment and common sense. I could very well be dead, writing this story from the spiritual realm.

My adrenaline is still pumping as I'm driving home after getting away from the cops in Sunnydale. I can feel the blood pulsating through my body, and my thoughts are scrambled. As I start to finally calm down, I replay the entire situation in my mind. *Man, that was crazy!*

As I drive toward the San Francisco and San Mateo county line, I become very vigilant. My run-in with the cops was in San Francisco, but I live in Daly City, which is only a few blocks away. To make it home safely, I have to cross the borderline. The Daly City Police Department is one of the strictest and most no-nonsense police departments around. They have zero tolerance for crime and a very high rate of issuing traffic citations and pulling people over for the most minor of reasons. I must be cautious.

As soon as I cross the county line, the Daly City Police start to follow me. *"Here we go again,"* I think, and then I realize I am violating not only the rule of law, but the rules of the streets: I don't have my seat belt on while transporting drugs; I'm wearing a baseball cap (perceived as part of the profile of a young drug dealer); and I have drugs on me—in Daly City, of all places.

After following me for two blocks, the cops turn their siren on. My mind starts racing wildly. *Should I take them on a chase? Do they know what just happened up the street? Is there an APB out for my car?* For some unknown reason, I decide to peacefully pull over, knowing that I have a valid driver's license and hoping they won't search me or the car.

As the officer gets out of his patrol car and walks to my vehicle, I look up and see that it's Officer Moreno. *Shit.* Officer Moreno is my archenemy who has been trying to bust me for over a year.

I ask calmly, "Why are you pulling me over, Officer?"

"Shut up and get out of the car, Malik."

My heart starts pounding. *Should I make a break for it?* I have two ounces of crack hidden in my underwear. *Maybe he won't search me.*

As cars drive past, nosy drivers rubberneck, watching me get questioned on the side of the road. Occupants of one car shoot me looks of disdain, shaking their heads as if to say, "I knew that boy was going to get busted." I try to keep a straight face to hide my embarrassment.

Without warning, I am thrown into the backseat of the police car. I haven't been searched yet and I still have the drugs on me. *Should I hide the drugs in* the backseat and hope that the cops don't find them? I decide to sling them out the window at the first opportunity. Which I did as soon as the officer turned his head for a split second to talk with his partner.

Several minutes pass. Two more police cars swerve up to the scene. The newly arrived cops snicker and stare, sizing me up as I sit stunned and limp in the backseat. They act like they just caught a great white shark. When being chased in Sunnydale, I felt like a runaway slave. Now I feel like a captured one. Whether I am right or wrong doesn't matter at the time; either way, I feel like I'm being harassed by a white police officer.

I anxiously watch the exchange between the officers, trying to get a sense of the situation by watching their body language. One of them finally turns toward me.

"Get out and put your hands behind your back. This looks like crack, Malik. I just found it underneath the police car."

I bark, "That ain't mine!"

"Tell it to the judge," one of them says.

As we drive to the police station, I think about the Spanish test I had at school today. I reminisce about basketball practice. I replay my run from the police. It has been a long and crazy day, clear evidence that I am no longer a "regular" teenager.

My next stop is the Daly City precinct holding cell. Police ask if I want to become a snitch. I play deaf and mute, which helps them get the message quickly. I insist they let me speak with a lawyer. The officer mocks me instead. "You are going to the big house, Malik." Before I know it, I am being booked into Hillcrest Juvenile Justice Center.

It's almost midnight when I get through the booking process. The intake officer guides me to a small room with a tan tile floor and plain gray walls. The room smells musty and dank and reminds me of an old folks' home.

I am drained and worn out mentally and physically. I stay awake for a while replaying the events of the day, but soon I am snoring.

When I open my eyes again, it's morning and a Mexican lady with big bushy hair is standing at my front door. "Wade, are you going to breakfast?" I reply no and go back to sleep. At 5 p. m., she reappears. "Wade, are you going to dinner?" "Yes."

I am now a juvenile ward of the state and also a soon-to-be felon.

This drama did absolutely nothing to deter me from being a king crook and dope dealer. Going to Juvenile Hall and then being sent to Glenwood Boys Ranch for four months had the exact opposite of what was intended. Instead of being deterred from criminal activity, I resolved to become a smarter and craftier criminal.

I actually thought that spending time in juvie would get me more respect when I got out. I had proven that I was not a snitch, that I was tough, and that I could fight. I had to represent San Francisco against those guys locked up from East Palo Alto, a rival city of sorts. In the back of my mind, I knew I couldn't go to prison because I was only sixteen. My worst-case scenario was being sent to California Youth Authority for five years. Even that threat didn't scare me because I thought if I spent time in YA—also known as "Gladiator School" back then—I would have even *more* respect when I got out.

My line of thinking made me bolder and brasher. My heart barely fit inside of my chest. My four-month sentence felt more like a rite of passage than punishment. After all, many of my friends had already been to the Hall and YA. I was actually late in getting to this milestone. Also, while in juvie I networked with other young rogues from nearby cities like East Palo Alto and San Mateo. While doing our "Ranch time," we made plans to hook up and continue our criminal activity together as soon as we hit the streets.

When I finally got out, I felt I had gotten my first stripes. Like I was in the Army. From the moment of my arrest, I moved up in rank from a private to a soon-to-be-sergeant in the military of the streets.

4
A FATHER'S IMPACT

I grew up without a steady father figure in my life even though my biological father lived a five-minute drive away from me and I eventually had a stepfather. Both were in my life inconsistently, and neither shared in the momentous events of my childhood and adolescence. Neither attended my youth basketball or football games; neither came to a parent-teacher conference, although my biological father did participate in my high school graduation.

My father, who died shortly after I returned from prison, was six foot two, handsome, and very charismatic. He was a neat dresser, naturally intelligent, and very street-smart. He was a quiet and pensive man who conducted himself with a lot of class and finesse. He was also a very hard worker. For over thirty years he operated a small, family-owned auto detail service called Wade's Service in San Rafael. He also traveled and toured the world extensively, living in Canada for some time, and in several cities throughout South America.

As a kid, whenever I was blessed to spend time with him, he would, in his wise yet unconventional way, teach me life lessons about character, integrity, humility, and the importance of being independent. One of the most important lessons he taught me was not to be judgmental and to be accepting of all people regardless of their ethnic, religious, or political backgrounds.

When I look back at my life, I reflect on the ways I could have greatly benefited from spending more quality time with my father, absorbing his knowledge, wisdom, and understanding. I made many mistakes along the way that could have been fatal, in part because I didn't have a steady well of wisdom to drink from. I remember one time in particular when I was sixteen, some guys from another neighborhood came to my high school looking to fight me over a girl. A little nervous and not knowing what to do, I went and got my first gun—a small nickel-plated .22—to protect myself. Fortunately, things turned out okay and I didn't shoot anyone or get myself hurt. However, if my father had been consistently in my life and guiding me, I believe I would have known how to handle that situation more diplomatically. That one key moment could have drastically changed my life's path forever. Other key moments *did* change my life's path forever.

I always wondered why I had to settle for a fraction of a father. No matter how I tried, I could not understand why he was not in my life more consistently. Although I couldn't explain it or even mentally process it, I knew I hadn't done anything to deserve being treated coldly and dealt with from a distance. Unfortunately, my relationship with my father was the rule and not the exception in the environment where I was raised. Most of my friends shared the same trauma from not having a steady father in their lives.

Many young men who grow up in inner cities all over the United States are conditioned to accept half of a dad—to be satisfied when our biological fathers merely acknowledge us in the smallest possible way. Many of us are enthusiastic and eager, willing to jump at the chance of a relationship, even when the father does something as small as say, "That is my son" to his friends. We're happy just because our father was willing to sign his name on the birth certificate and grateful to have a "holiday daddy," who comes around only for holiday celebrations and other special occasions. Obviously, none of those actions represent the essence of fatherhood, yet many of us don't understand the magnitude of how we are ultimately affected, traumatized, and emotionally and mentally wounded until we grow older and understand life on a deeper level.

My father didn't sign my birth certificate. In retrospect, this was indicative of how our relationship would play out over the remainder of my life. His refusal to sign my birth certificate would be a consistent source of resentment and frustration for me over the years. Although I consciously tried to suppress negative thoughts about the issue, as a young man I would occasionally have emotional eruptions with authority figures such as teachers and coaches—and even my mother.

I strongly believe much of my bad attitude and temper outbursts can be attributed to my feelings of anger and animosity because I did not feel 100 percent accepted by my father. I concealed those feelings well but carried them with me for many years. This was clearly displacement and projection; I transferred my anger and inner ill feelings toward my father onto other things or people who were more accessible and who made a safer target. From what I have experienced and witnessed, I am certain that many young men across America have very similar feelings. The phenomenon of absent or distant fathers transcends color lines, class lines, and gender lines; it is by no means specific to the African American community.

Having "half of a dad" or a "holiday daddy" does not contribute to healthy growth and development for any boy or young man. Ultimately, and just as importantly, creating such a relationship can also negatively impact the father, resulting in self-destructive and harmful behaviors and sometimes leading to unintended consequences such as mental health problems, drug abuse, alcoholism, incarceration, abuse of women, violent behavior, or multiple children by multiple women out of wedlock. The destruction of essential, foundational relationships between father and son causes a lot of pain, anger, and confusion in many directions. Unfortunately, there is no cure-all to correct this puzzling phenomenon; its roots are historical and systemic.

I have spoken with men who have strangely bragged about being "holiday daddies." They boast and huff and puff about how many gifts they buy their children for Christmas or their birthdays. They brag and beat their chests with a powerful closed fist when they talk about big birthday bashes and parties with bouncy houses, clowns, and petting zoos. Some of them say *cheese* for the camera, show all thirty-two teeth, and smile proudly when they talk about the new pair of Air Jordans or new iPhones they bought the sons they had not physically seen in years! Could these be guilt gifts? It's ironic that many of these same men rarely offer an explanation for why they suddenly and unexpectedly disappear from their children's lives for long periods—sometimes even decades.

Unfortunately and ironically—to keep it real and honest—at points in my life I've resembled the exact model of the absent father that I am rebuking. Prison is not a legitimate excuse for having missed thirteen straight years of my daughter's life. I left when she slept in a crib and returned when she was in high school. It's painful to consider the progress I sacrificed in our relationship.

All boys need a father figure. Like all young men, I searched for and sought the validation and reassuring hand of a strong and steady male presence, which I believe to be absolutely essential for the emotional well-being of a child. Although having a father may not guarantee successful life outcomes in and of itself, according to a 2013 study conducted by Kimberly Howard and Richard V. Reeves at the Center on Children and Families at the Brookings Institution, a two-parent household at the very least provides for higher family total income and better financial stability.

Young men make continuous attempts to discover themselves. All young men go through this process on some level at some point in their lives—Black or White; rich or poor; with or without a father in the home. However, a boy with no father present is sure to experience a very difficult task to discover self. We all start as the same humble caterpillar in a cocoon of ignorance, but we could all use some help learning how to shed that cocoon and grow our wings.

The journey of finding myself consisted of many different things: beginning sexual explorations and relationships with girls; developing an educational identity (*Did I want to be cool or smart? Could I be both?*); shaping my cultural identity; and trying to understand my own masculinity. Fortunately for me, I always performed well in school and had an innate love for learning. Based on my mother's Black consciousness and awareness, I had a strong African American cultural identity. And I was never confused about my masculinity or sexuality; I was always sexually attracted to girls and women only.

My relationship with my father didn't really start to develop until I was a teenager. By that time, however, I had already developed a personality, a character, and a belief system regarding how I wanted to live my life. I wasn't necessarily a bad or super rebellious kid or teenager, but I had some glaring gaps in my overall understanding of life because I did not have a knowledgeable male figure in my life on a consistent basis to help me put things into proper perspective. This was particularly true when I was young and my mind was still developing, my personality and character were taking shape, and my habits and patterns (good and bad) were forming.

Generally, we are all products of our environments, our experiences, and decisions that we make. There have been truly amazing individuals who have overcome the issue of not having a father and gone on to do great things. Men such as former President Barack

Obama, rappers Jay-Z and Tupac Shakur, baseball player Alex Rodriguez, entertainer Kanye West, and civil rights icon Malcolm X are just a few examples. However, the vast majority of men without a father will at some point experience some turbulence due to this absence. Although many of the men mentioned above went on to do great and wondrous things, we don't know how their lack of a father has ultimately impacted them throughout their own personal lives.

I definitely do not blame my life outcomes on my mostly absent father. Yet, although it is not the sole reason for my questionable choices and decisions, I cannot underestimate how much the absence of a reliable father in my formative years played a key role in the path of my life.

5
HUBRIS

As I said earlier, my time in Juvenile Hall did little to put me on a different path. Neither did the knowledge that the consequences changed when I became an adult; the penalties and drug laws that loomed over me then were long and stiff. By that time, I was being sought by the police and stalked by human hyenas: kidnappers. Both forms of attention were unwelcome.

One Saturday morning when I was nineteen, I went outside to empty the trash and was stung by a surprise attack. Two men in black ski masks tackled me and pointed a 12-gauge shotgun against the nape of my neck. Instinctively, I looked toward the kitchen window for my six-year-old sister, Mimi, and found her watching in shock. The sad and scared look on her face gave me superhuman strength, allowing me to aggressively turn the tables on the would-be kidnappers.

With the shotgun nestled against my neck, I nimbly twisted and contorted my body like a professional wrestler as the kidnappers and I wildly tussled for control of the shotgun. Stumbling and scrapping in the mud, I hung onto the gun with a death grip, coming close to taking control, but it was two against one and I couldn't overpower them both. After a few more deadlocked seconds, they were forced to retreat, running to a waiting van down the street with two other would-be abductors. I quickly ran into the house to grab my pistol, but they were long gone.

Because I was constantly under threat due to the position I had put myself in, I grew fangs. I became hard-hearted and unforgiving, and I kept a pistol and a box of 9-millimeter shells either on me or very close to me at all times. I trusted nobody, and my "Spidey senses" stayed on high alert. After the near kidnapping, I knew I had to rearrange my entire program quickly. It was a life-and-death situation. There was no time for procrastinating when dealing with kidnappers and hit men.

I made some immediate changes to my daily routine, and that very same day, I bought my mother a car so she would not have to walk alone to the bus stop on her way to work. Within weeks, I had moved my mother and both of my sisters into a safer neighborhood. This ability to use the money I was making to protect my family from the violence born of the way I was making the money was a part of what kept me in the vicious cycle.

My mother had a strong idea that I was selling drugs for several years before this attempted kidnapping, but after this incident, there was no doubt in her mind. Because she was worried for the safety of her family, her spiritual beliefs and her own personal judgment of my activities would have to be put aside in order to address the immediate concerns. Bottom line, I was a dope dealer with enemies, and we would have to move immediately if we all wanted to live. Moving also gave me the best chance to avoid committing murder. Although she didn't condone or encourage my drug dealing, I believe my mother, like many single mothers in urban America—and particularly those raising young Black men—at some point had become mentally tired and emotionally exhausted from raising three children without any emotional support from a husband or a responsible man around.

So like others who find themselves in similar situations with sons in the streets, my mother unwillingly accepted the fact that she could no longer give me a spanking or some other paltry punishment to get me to comply. And she knew she could not call on my father for any support because he had never been much of a support.

At nineteen, I was no longer living in her house, although I would come over every day to bring my baby sister home from day care. I had a couple of different apartments by that time and was taking care of myself. There was very little that my mother could do to control me, and I kept sinking deeper and deeper into hustling, even after many close calls. The attempted kidnapping made it clear that my bluff would eventually be called again. If I did nothing to retaliate, others would stand in line to test me to see if I had the heart to kill. Would I get executed or would I be the executioner? This wasn't normally my way of operating, but kissing the barrel of a 12-gauge will swiftly change one's outlook on life. There is a fine line between what a man is and what a man can become.

What I was becoming was a man who was getting busted on the regular for firearm beefs because I would rather be caught with a gun than without, given my concerns about being tested by my enemies. In a relatively short period of time, I was busted on three separate occasions for gun possession. Each time I got a high-powered lawyer, got bailed out quickly, and was sentenced to probation.

The fourth time I was charged by the Feds. This fourth infraction meant I could technically be charged as what the Feds called an "armed career criminal," which carried a sentence of fifteen years to life as an appetizer. Typically, my money could "buy" a state case and make it go away. But the Feds? Well, that was a different story.

But before that fourth charge occurred, I was working as a twenty-one-year-old drug dealer at the top of my game. I was jet setting from state to state, in and out of the airport every few days—flying to another city to do another deal.

My entire drug career was a contradiction to the dealer image. I didn't fit into the many media stereotypes of the super violent drug kingpin who leaves body bags piled up all over the city. Media depictions of drug dealers tend to focus on the sensational, sexy exploits of the drug game; they seldom address the negatives, such as prison, depression, death, and life on the run. I considered myself one of many Americans from poor backgrounds who sought wealth to pull ourselves out of poverty. In my mind, I was no different than Al Capone; we both considered ourselves to be natural businessmen—entrepreneurs who understood and excelled at the game of capitalism.

When I started my criminal career at the age of fifteen, my goals were simple: first make $10,000. Then $100,000. Then $1,000,000. And so on. My mentality was to hustle hard and make all the money I could without getting life in prison. But, ultimately, the plan was flawed and destined to fail because I didn't have an exit strategy.

I made a stark gamble no matter which way you cut it.

6
TROUBLE IN PITTSBURGH

"Eric is snitching! We've been set up!"

It's PD Mack on the phone.

"The Feds and the DEA just raided and ransacked the house! They have the city roadblocked looking for us. We had to run one of their cars off the road in a high-speed chase! We gotta get the hell out of here. I can't talk right now! I'll call you back!"

Click.

Something had gone horribly wrong in Pittsburgh. PD was usually calm and composed.

As I hang up, I hear ear-piercing sirens. All I could see is a future of steel penitentiary bars. Something is tugging and twisting my intestines. I have to find the nearest toilet to take a seat.

For the rest of the day I wait for the return phone call, even though I have a funny feeling the call might not come. I hear nothing as I anxiously pace in my hotel suite, sneaking peeks from behind the curtains, watching out for the Feds.

My phone finally rings the next day. I eagerly answer. "Hello?!"

"You have a collect call from PD Mack."

"I accept!"

"The Feds got us," PD says when he comes on the line. "They are threatening us with twenty to life."

"Damn!" I'm shocked.

"Eric told them everything. He's an informant. It's ugly."

"What do you need me to do?"

"Get me and J-Run a lawyer and get out of town as soon as possible. When the Feds catch you, you'll be facing a life sentence."

I hung up the phone and sat speechless for a moment, pondering my next move. I was in Los Angeles and would have to quickly wrap up my business and make it back home to San Francisco to operate on familiar footing. It was time to make some moves to pay for lawyers and prepare for a life on the run.

The previous couple of months had been difficult. In addition to close calls with the police in Pittsburgh, we had run into trouble in West Virginia and Louisville, Kentucky. Now the Feds were hot on my trail in LA. I had to carefully contemplate my next gambit. My next move had to be my best one. I had to be a master chess player.

As I was tying up loose ends in LA, I ran into more bad luck. While I was driving in Beverly Hills with a friend, the police pulled us over and searched the car. I feared the Feds had somehow tracked me to LA. As the police searched the car, they found a designer leather jacket in the trunk with a $7,000 price tag still on it that I had bought from my friend. Before we knew it, my friend and I were slung to the sidewalk, arrested, and booked into the Beverly Hills jail on charges of receiving stolen property.

Dread started to set in. I wasn't sure whether the Feds had anything to do with my arrest or if it was tied to the investigation in Pittsburgh. I was worried about getting out in time to get my friends a lawyer. I was the only one with access to our money and assets. I was hoping that the Feds had not put a hold on me.

Damn. What am I gonna do? I was scheduled to go to court the next morning. I anxiously paced the small holding cell all night. All day and half the night I urgently made back-to-back phone calls and sent emergency messages. I called my lawyer in San Francisco and told him to find out whether the Feds had issued an arrest warrant for me.

I was able to call back several tense hours later. No warrant yet, my lawyer said, but one could be issued any minute. He advised me to relax and prepare to go to court the next morning. I barked back, "Relax?! I may be going to prison and you are going home to your wife and kids!"

My lawyer suddenly had another client on the other line and couldn't talk anymore. I slammed the phone down in frustration. It was a long and lonely night in that tiny concrete cell.

The next morning came. As the deputy called off names one by one to go to court, my breathing got a little heavier. If my name wasn't called I would have to stay in jail, and that could give the Feds more time to track me down.

Suddenly, the deputy hollered, "Wade, you are being released. All charges are being dropped because the DA has insufficient evidence to charge you." I couldn't believe it. I eagerly walked toward the door. *Now the chase is* really *on.*

I was fresh out of jail, but the police had taken everything: my cell phone, my keys, my money. I managed to make a phone call to get some money wired through Western Union so I could get out of

LA. I made it back to my hotel suite, although I was afraid the place would be crawling with the Feds. I slipped back into my hotel room without being detected, quickly packed my clothes, and soon was on a flight headed back to San Francisco.

When I got back to San Francisco, the real work began. It was Thursday and the lawyer wanted $40,000 by Monday. I had to round up the cash, purchase a cashier's check, and send it via overnight mail. While I was scrambling to get everything in order—which was more difficult than usual because I had been living in LA for a while and was a little disoriented—I was in constant communication with PD Mack on the phone.

Considering that he was in jail and facing twenty to life, his spirits were relatively good. Although distressed, he didn't panic. He trusted that I would take care of the business.

The saga in Pittsburgh had started about a year earlier when I traveled there for the first time with a friend named Shooter. Shooter and I had met previously in New York when I went there searching for new drug markets. He was a prototypical New Yorker, aggressive and always hustling. He was a physically intimidating dude, about six-three and 230 solid pounds with a raspy New York accent—stout and stocky but built like Mike Tyson; his mere presence made you notice him. Shooter was a bulldozer. He cleared the path for me in Pittsburgh like an offensive lineman.

Shooter took me to Pittsburgh at the request of a friend who needed a California connection. I was understandably mistrustful and suspicious of everybody, including his friend. Shooter was well-known and knew everybody in town. He had rock star status. Pittsburgh, despite being considered an East Coast city, had a Midwest vibe to it. It wasn't as fast-paced as other East Coast cities, like New York or Washington, D.C., but you couldn't get caught napping either. The criminal element was wide awake, and the murder rate was rising quickly.

Pittsburgh, the "Steel City," was what some people call grimy—an old, gothic-looking city that had a dark and depressing spirit. The closing of the old steel mills and factories that had made Pittsburgh famous left huge, dilapidated and decaying factories and shuttered manufacturing plants that stretched for blocks and were eyesores on the city landscape. Entire neighborhoods, like Braddock and McKeesport, looked deserted and desolate.

The city's local economy was in the toilet, but the drug game was at full throttle, producing a thriving underground economy. Depression from the loss of steel mill and manufacturing jobs soaked the city and bled into the people. Thousands of drug addicts roamed the streets like zombies in the *Night of the Living Dead*.

However, this depressing city looked good to me because it presented an excellent opportunity to quickly become a millionaire! I felt like a newly arrived immigrant to the United States, fleeing a third-world country with big dreams.

When I arrived in Pittsburgh, the people automatically gave me respect and were intrigued because I was from California. But the local police were on high alert because Crips and Bloods from California were at that point fanning out across the country and setting up new factions and affiliates in almost every neighborhood in the United States. People automatically assumed that I belonged to one of those groups. I did not.

Shooter and I were there for one reason: to make money. Our goal was to take over "the game" in an entire neighborhood. We had a very specific, calculated plan. We weren't there to party or make friends with the locals or to hang out with girls; it was strictly business. Pittsburgh was a sweet spot, and the neighborhood we targeted was a potential million-dollar operation. I couldn't wait to get started.

First I had to meet the who's who of the gangland. I met all of the "ghetto stars"—the biggest dealer in town, the kidnappers, the stick-up kids, and the killers. And of course there were plenty of women who wanted to taste the forbidden fruit from out of town. I was a fresh-faced twenty-year-old, full of ambition and a lot of nerve.

After a couple of days of scouting, surveying the land, doing homework on the different players of the game, and learning the logistics of the city, I was ready to get busy. I did what business leaders call a SWOT analysis: strengths, weaknesses, opportunities, and threats. I listed a couple of strengths: I had the product and I had it for a cheaper price than they were currently paying; I wasn't from Pittsburgh, which made me a mystery that they couldn't figure out; and I could keep them off balance by being unpredictable. As far as opportunities, I could quickly become a millionaire if my plan was executed properly. My main weakness? I didn't know who might be an informant working with the Feds or the local police. Threats included gun-toting kidnappers and stick-up kids who took offense to out-of-towners like Shooter and me. After the SWOT analysis, we also ran a competitive analysis—an intense study of the competition.

Once the foundation was laid, our launch went relatively smoothly. Business was booming. It was the perfect example of the law of supply and demand, as they say in economics. Things ran like a well-oiled machine, and we were getting new clients and customers every day. After a while, as things moved along and profits increased, Shooter and I chose to part ways. I stayed in Pittsburgh, and he moved on to set up an operation in another state. We remained the best of friends.

But when Shooter left, I was out there exposed and alone, without the team that was needed to run a fine-tuned operation. Soon I would need reinforcements to assist with the day-to-day operations and share in the profits. A few weeks later, a new "starting five" flew in from California. The team format allowed us to expand into other markets in nearby cities and towns.

The first day the squad arrived, I gave them a scouting report and shared the game plan while we drove around the city, keenly sizing up the neighborhood. As we started to network and interact with several of the known and reputable gangsters, I sensed there was some funk and fresh tension with some of the locals. They had gotten used to seeing me alone and were comfortable with me, but they didn't know or trust these new faces.

Now, as I drove by, I received threatening frowns instead of the smiles and waves I had received when operating alone. One day a local pulled me to the side and told me to be careful; some of the neighborhood stick-up men were plotting a robbery and were offended by "the other California dudes" I had brought in. The guy who was telling me this had a treacherous reputation and played with pistols like they were water guns; I didn't take him lightly. But I immediately recalled that "the dog who brings a bone carries a bone with him." What was his angle? He became a "frenemy."

After a few minor incidents, my team started to get in a groove and things started to move along smoothly. We operated discreetly and didn't bring attention to ourselves or flaunt the fact that we were from out of town. After a while, we blended right into the community; some of us even adopted the local dress code of the commoner: Carhartt hoodies and knit beanie hats.

Working as a team, we were able to split up the roles and responsibilities. Our job descriptions were clearly defined, and we were as efficient as any successful small business. As far as the team was concerned everyone was equal. We were all strong leaders and good managers, all level-headed and willing to sacrifice for the greater good of the team: M-O-N-E-Y! However, as we aggressively expanded into new markets such as Braddock and McKeesport, Pennsylvania, we were sowing seeds that would eventually flower into a federal indictment.

We didn't know that there was a hateful whispering campaign taking place among the local folks—a Machiavellian movement to get us out of the way by any means necessary. As we found out later, several individuals started to turn on us and became FBI informants as jealousy and envy saturated the environment. One wrong move could result in death or a life sentence. I had been responsible for putting many of the pieces in place and some major mistakes in judgment allowed us to be infiltrated and ultimately betrayed.

Because I had become cocky and overconfident, I lost focus and was to blame when we took a huge financial loss that cost us $90,000 in revenues. Weeks later, we experienced back-to-back losses of $56,000. This was the beginning of the end, as we took on the shared mind-set of a chronic gambler who continuously loses, tries to get it all back too quickly, but eventually goes on to lose it all.

This horrible turn of events would end up being the forewarning to something that ultimately would end in tragedy for the entire team. I felt guilty because it was mostly my fault for trusting the locals too much. I broke one of the golden rules of drug dealing: trust no one.

7
THE CHASE IS ON!!!

My legs give out from underneath me. Dizzy and dazed, I stumble and sit on the curb and try to recover. For a fraction of a second, I feel as if I had been knocked out. I am standing outside my lawyer's office in downtown San Francisco, where I have just been told that the United States Attorney's office has indicted me on federal drug charges. They are seeking the maximum sentence—life in federal prison.

It is like being told that I have stage four terminal cancer with weeks to live. I have just turned twenty-two. *Damn. What do I do next?*

Within a few hours, I am on a plane, hoping to flee the country. But I can't come up with the documents I need—a fake ID, a driver's license, and a new Social Security card—so I stop and restrategize. I can't cross the Canadian border just yet, so I head for Seattle, just a few hours from the border, to plan my next move.

By nightfall I am in Seattle. It's my first time in that city, and its natural beauty surprises me. Although it's growing dark when my plane lands, I can still see beautiful Mount Rainier National Park and its breathtaking white snowcapped mountains. I immediately feel a little more at ease. The air in Seattle smells fresh and clean from a recent rainstorm, and the vibe seems calm and low-key.

"*This might be a sweet spot to lay low for a while.*"

After landing in Seattle, I knew that I needed to figure out how to quickly make some money, so the next day I drove around in a rental car getting familiar with the city and looking for "entrepreneurial opportunities." I quickly came to the conclusion that I'd need to develop a plan to infiltrate the local drug market. It was a super risky proposition, but my back was against the wall, and—after all—I was still a greedy drug dealer. Old habits die hard.

I had been selling dope in other states and different cities, so I was confident my plan could work. I wasn't too worried about learning the local landscape of the drug market, but I was concerned about getting a new case, considering I was already running from the Feds.

The first thing I did was reconnect with a woman who had been a former accomplice and crime partner. We had been in a relationship in San Francisco, and she had recently moved to Seattle. She was a ruthless and coldhearted hustler, rougher than most men I knew, and I knew I could trust her to watch my back because she had a sharp mind and a swift wit and packed a pistol in her purse instead of lipstick. Just what I needed.

Once we got together, we rented an apartment in a nice quiet neighborhood and purchased a low-key car. I made some business phone calls back to California and got the number of a local contact who was in Tacoma, Washington, a small city about thirty miles south of Seattle.

When I got to Tacoma I drove around to scout potential areas to set up my operation. Tacoma was a slower-paced city with a country-like setting. It had the look and feel of a Midwest manufacturing town, mostly populated by blue-collar workers and regular working-class folks. I had to be careful because if I didn't move sharply I would stick out and bring attention to myself, which could attract the Feds or local rivals. Tacoma had a growing gang culture and local gang members always loved to make an example of out-of-towners coming into their market. I refused to be prey for the predators.

I drive to the house of my new Tacoma contact, a woman named Chuck. Her house is the neighborhood hideout—gangbanger headquarters. From outside, the house looks run down and raggedy, and the front lawn is full of rotten crabgrass. An old Cadillac with four flat tires is parked haphazardly on the street. As I get out of my car, a couple of pit bulls snarl at me, foaming at the mouth as if dinner had just arrived.

"Man, this might be shady."

On high alert, I walk in the house and find five or six members of the notorious Tacoma Crips gang in the living room. I immediately feel the power of their presence. They all have on the Crips uniform: blue hooded sweatshirts, blue Chuck Taylor tennis shoes, blue Dickies pants, and blue bandanas in their back pockets. When I walk in, the music suddenly stops, the drinking stops, and the dice game comes to a screeching halt.

Everybody looks at me mystified, as if I were an

alien. The room suddenly feels like a sauna. One abruptly jumps up and aggressively asks, "Where you from, Cuz?" As a defense mechanism, I ignore him, and walk to the back of the house to talk business privately with Chuck. There is no need to address him. I am here to make money, not to gangbang.

It seems like all the gang members in the house have a gun visibly showing or bulging in their waistbands. I don't have a gun, but I damn sure bluff like I do. I walk in boldly to prevent any attempts to intimidate me. I'm wearing a blue Seattle Seahawks hooded sweatshirt and some blue Girbaud jeans, simulating their dress code to imply that I might be an ally from an affiliate faction or clique of Crips from another neighborhood. Although I'm not a Crip, my clothes could buy me some time to get familiar with this group and put them at ease or—as we say in the streets—rock them asleep. It's important for me to camouflage myself and blend in, as it's part of my scheme to make them feel comfortable doing business with me.

Once Chuck and I finish talking, I turn to leave the house. The silence echoes as the Crips size me up, sniffing for the scent of fear and slicing me with their eyes. I reflect back that same silence as my source of strength. *The Art of War* had taught me well. I walk out of the house safely.

After about a week, I had made some connections with some of the main shot callers from the Crips, and I was ready to do business. I made some arrangements in California to have the product brought to Seattle, and I was ready to operate within a few days. My goal was to make as much money as I could as fast as I could, then sneak across the border to Canada before another federal investigation started.

Things started off relatively smoothly. Even though I was doing business with hardcore gang members and killers, they were also serious businessmen who wanted to make money, so they didn't have a problem working with someone who wasn't a gang member. We both had an unspoken respect for the number one rule and principle of the criminal code of conduct: M-O-N-E-Y.

However, as time went on, I heard the Crips were plotting to kidnap or kill me. I called a meeting with Capone, one of the Crips' main enforcers. As part of my strategy, I went straight to "the killing fields" and met them on their turf, right in the notorious Hilltop section of Tacoma. I showed up to the meeting with a firm look on my face, pretending I had major backing. They arrived four deep in a blue '64 Chevy Impala, but my strong body language showed them that I wasn't intimidated—even though their scowls and their reputation could have intimidated a pit bull.

I immediately addressed the accusations of the rumored robbery and kidnapping. First, I quietly but firmly told them I was at an advantage because I was not from the area and could easily disappear after exacting retribution. Their families had lived in the area for generations; I knew where their grandparents, mothers, and children lived. They knew nothing of mine. Then I reminded them that unnecessary bloodshed would benefit neither side. Capone reluctantly nodded his head in agreement as he stared through me and rubbed the "Killer" tattoo over his eyebrow.

Ultimately, I was able to reason with them—convincing them that I represented an "economic opportunity"—and that any talk of killing me prevented them from feeding their families. The meeting ended peacefully, and we continued to do business without further problem. Meeting with them was a risky but shrewd stunt on my part, and it was necessary to keep them guessing. This particular chess game ended in a stalemate.

Periodically, I would call San Francisco to ask my lawyer if he had heard anything new on my case. He always replied, "There is nothing new and, as your attorney, for the record, I have to advise you to turn yourself in to the authorities." Click. I would hang up every time.

Once, I snapped back at him, "Would you turn yourself in?" I couldn't imagine the thought of willingly turning myself in to face a life sentence.

After a couple of months, I started to wrap up my business in Tacoma and plot my next move. I had to do so carefully because I couldn't let the guys I was doing business with know their supply would be cut off soon. I had to ease my hand out of the lion's mouth.

A couple of people owed me huge sums of money; one guy owed me over $25,000. I had to get my money while manipulating them into thinking our business arrangement would continue for the foreseeable future. I handled die-hard drug dealers, and especially hardcore gang members, like feral animals that could suddenly snap and viciously attack at any moment. So I feigned empathy and understanding, aiming to make them feel completely comfortable. But all along, I knew that when all the money was collected, I would disappear into thin air.

It's about 4:00 a. m., pitch black outside. I'm driving north on Highway 5, headed to Canada. The road is eerily empty; all I hear is the engine humming and my thoughts racing. I breathe a huge sigh of relief to be leaving Tacoma and Seattle. I know I'm fortunate to make it out of there with my life and without catching a murder or getting any new federal drug charges.

I am keeping my fingers crossed that the FBI won't "pile on" with new charges from other cities if I ever get arrested because I know the Feds have a five-year period to bring an indictment. And once charged by the Feds, the indictment never expires; there is no statute of limitations. The clock on the criminal complaint ticks forever until the time of capture.

As I get closer to the border, my heart starts pounding. I repeatedly rehearse my story just in case a super-cop border-crossing agent quizzes me. Crossing the border is risky, but necessary. I can't stay in the United States; my trail is too hot. The FBI has my house back in San Francisco under constant surveillance, and they are following my girl and my father, hoping one of them will lead them to me. To make matters worse, I recently left a hot trail in Tacoma. I *have* to get some distance between that life sentence and me!

Dribbles of sweat form on my nose. *Damn, I am sweating at the wrong time!* As I slowly pull up to the border crossing, the pudgy, bespectacled crossing agent stares at me and abruptly tells me to turn off the car. I am irritated at being singled out and, quite frankly, scared. But I reluctantly put the car in park.

I try to stay calm, but the agent then tells me to pull to the side of the road. I nearly panic and punch the gas but manage to hold it together. Once I get out of the car, he stares me up and down and instructs me to walk into the immigration office. *If they run my fingerprints, things could get ugly.*

The lady at the desk appears suspicious and asks me for ID. I give her my fake ID, which she scrutinizes to see if my face matches the picture. She abruptly leaves to speak with her supervisor. She's gone for only a few seconds, but it feels like hours. My entire life is in her hands. If she gets doubtful and detains me for further questioning, I might die in prison!

The supervisor leisurely walks over to me and says, "Sir, we would like to search your car." As they walk out to the car, my stomach twists in knots. I wonder if they are suspicious about the car registration. I feel light-headed as they carefully comb through the car with two giant black German shepherds. I helplessly look through the window of the immigration office as the dogs bark wildly. It feels like things are going from bad to worse.

The border agent walks towards me, the dogs yanking violently on the leash. He looks at me coldly, pauses, then abruptly says, "You're clean sir. Enjoy your vacation in Vancouver."

Trying to conceal my nerves, I politely take back my keys, get in the car, drive across the border, and ride off into the fog of Vancouver, Canada. I don't know where I'm going or what I'll do next, but there's a strong possibility that I will never see the United States again.

8
THE PHONE CALL

I suspiciously peeked over my shoulder, weaving in and out of foot traffic, as I walked several blocks to a phone booth. I was being extremely careful, wary of any peculiar activity, making sure that no one was following me.

"Hello?" I heard my fiancée's voice at the other end of the line.

"Did you make sure that you weren't followed by the Feds?"

"Yes it's clear," she reassured me. "PD Mack just called. He said he went to federal court this morning and was sentenced to twenty-seven years in federal prison, and your other friend, J-Run, was sentenced to twenty-two years."

"WHAT?!" I barked in disbelief.

"He said that the Feds have you identified as one of the leaders of a cocaine distribution conspiracy from California to Pennsylvania. Whenever they catch you, you're facing life in Federal prison. I gotta go! I'll call you in a few days!"

I hang up the phone and stand still, speechless. My mind momentarily goes blank.

Then I begin to think about my decisions over the past twenty-one years. *Damn! I fucked up this time.*

I slowly exit the phone booth and start sluggishly walking in complete confusion. I distrust everyone I see. Are they all staring at me? Do they all know that the Feds are looking for me? My bowels bubble.

Where will I be twenty years from now?

I aimlessly float around downtown Vancouver, trying to distract myself from thoughts of going to Leavenworth federal penitentiary for the rest of my life. I watch the hustle and bustle of the crowds—people rushing to and from work; cabs zipping in and out of traffic.

I am barely conscious of the pouring rain, except to think of it as symbolic of my present circumstances: damp and depressing. The harder it rains, the more depressed I become.

I feel totally isolated. I can't call anyone to talk about my dilemma because the phones back in California are tapped. People passing me on the street don't seem to be giving me a second glance. I must look composed on the outside. Internally, I am emotionally shipwrecked.

I walk to Kitsilano Beach, sit in the sand and watch the waves come ashore. I let my mind stray, but it keeps returning to the same questions. *Will I ever see my family again? Will I eventually die in prison?*

I walked around downtown Vancouver in a haze of dark confusion for several more hours. I felt as if I was blindfolded and walking in a huge endless circle; I felt as if my life was meaningless. After wearily walking around for hours, I eventually went home and instantly fell into a deep sleep.

When I woke the next morning, I knew my new life was about to begin. Not just a life as a fugitive, but a fugitive running from a life sentence. The Feds had set the bar high when they sentenced my friends. They had called our bluff. They made an example of my friends, and they clearly wanted my head on a platinum platter. I was the next man up to be marched to the guillotine to be beheaded.

Soon I would need to flee Vancouver and travel to another part of Canada. Vancouver was too close to the U.S. border, and I couldn't risk the Feds coming across attempting to extradite me back. Plus, Vancouver was less than 1 percent Black. Blending in was impossible. I felt as visible as Shaquille O'Neal walking around China. I eventually decided to pack up and hit the highway. I didn't know exactly where I was going, but Vancouver was too close to a life sentence.

Driving through the snowcapped mountains of British Columbia, my mind drifted. I unsuccessfully tried to suppress my thoughts, but four letters continuously popped into my head: L-I-F-E.

With hundreds of miles of empty road ahead of me, there was plenty of time for me to think and reflect. My eyes burned from staring through the front windshield for countless hours. As time passed, I became extremely pensive, analyzing my entire life—past, present, and unknown future. I thought about my past: *Where did I go wrong?* My present: *How will I survive and take care of myself today?* My future: *What will happen to me? Can I run forever? Do I want to?*

I reflected on the potential of one phone call or conversation to change an entire life. One moment, one occurrence, one happening can capsize your entire world. No man or woman knows what tomorrow will bring. As humans, how do we react to being told that we have cancer? Or that our spouse is filing for divorce? That a partner has cheated, a child has just committed suicide, or a parent has passed away? How do we deal if someone close to us is killed? How do we react to the news that we are facing a life sentence in prison?

We are all emotionally fragile and can snap and lose it at any moment. As I firmly gripped the steering wheel and pressed the pedal a little bit harder, I felt that my time was running out.

I had been driving nonstop for hours; I was starting to see double, and the road became blurry as I grew drowsy. It was a lonely stretch of highway, and it seemed that I was the only car on the road. In actuality, I probably *was* the only Black person driving on this highway for hundreds of miles. I barely stopped for gas because I worried about being singled out by the police or nosy hicks.

I finally decided to stop driving when I couldn't take it anymore. I was physically and emotionally drained and getting delirious. I stopped in a sparsely populated town in southwest Alberta. I immediately felt like a foreigner in this place where I saw almost no one on the streets. I drove around for a while—trying to get a feel for the town. I found a hotel on an isolated back road that was conveniently hidden behind some trees and hedging. Perfect.

Once I checked into the room, I quickly surveyed the perimeter, silently walking through the hotel, looking for potential flaws in the security system. As I conducted my walk-through, I visualized different escape scenarios if my cover was blown or the Feds unexpectedly showed up. I scoped out all potential getaway routes, including the windows, balconies, and roof. I checked the phone line, listening for suspicious sounds to make sure it wasn't tapped.

For the first couple of days, I laid low. I only left the room to get fast food. With a Black population of zero percent, it was impossible to be a chameleon in this town. A six-two, 210-pound Black man was as noticeable as someone strolling down the street naked. When I walked to the store, I felt like all eyes were on me. When spoken to, I stayed low-key and answered with a fake smile. I didn't want to engage in long conversation. I didn't want anyone to be able to positively ID me.

After several weeks of being on the lookout for suspicious activity and undercover agents, I started to ease my way into the city. I went to local restaurants and bookstores and took casual walks in the park. I would typically try to wait until it was dark outside before I started my routine. As the weeks went on, I became slightly less cautious with my counter-surveillance.

However, I started to get suspicious when the hotel manager started knocking on my hotel room door regularly to see if "I needed towels or anything." She also began to unexpectedly come to my room to "check on me" or see "if I wanted to talk." This struck me as strange. One day I came back to the room from an early morning jog and discovered that the manager was in my room "getting the laundry." I clearly startled her when I came in, but she played it cool and left without a fuss. I immediately got suspicious, so I packed up and was back on the road just minutes later.

I was able to make occasional phone calls to my girl back home, and I learned my family and friends thought that I was doing okay, that I was successfully hiding from the FBI. Through the grapevine, they heard that I was in hiding somewhere in Canada. I got the sense that they believed I was living a daring and exciting life as an international fugitive. They completely misunderstood. Although I was not imprisoned physically, I was a prisoner of my own conscience.

9
THE FUGITIVE

My life was unstable and unpredictable. I had no dreams. I had no goals. I was unable to plan for my future. I wanted to buy a home, but I couldn't stay in one place too long. I wanted to raise children, but what kind of father could I be while I was on the run from the Feds? I wish I could have clicked my heels three times like Dorothy in *The Wizard of Oz*, chanted, "There's no place like home," and switched back to a normal life. But that was the movies and this was real life.

I was in a mental straitjacket. The pressure and heavy weight of stress and anxiety from constantly watching my back were starting to wear me down. I started to worry about the irregular heartbeats and palpitations I was regularly experiencing.

Weeks of living on the run turned into months turned into years. I was constantly on the move, traveling from town to city, from province to state, from country to country. I was tired of secretly zigzagging across the continent, of smuggling myself in and out of the country and back and forth across the border. I was tired of evading government officials and ducking FBI "Wanted" lists in the post office. Today I am in Vancouver; tomorrow, Calgary; the next week, Edmonton; then Winnipeg, Manitoba; and so on. There was no rest. Would it ever end?

Things felt surreal and dreamlike, but it wasn't a dream. It was an intensely real existence. My life was a game of chess, a series of strategically preplanned moves. Nobody outside of my hometown of San Francisco really knew who I was, and nobody in my hometown of San Francisco really knew where I was. I lived and lurked in the shadows. My life was desperately real, but at the same time, I felt like I was a phantom or, worse, like I didn't exist at all.

I needed to see a doctor for the irregular heartbeats, but I chose not to because I didn't want to identify myself. The cutting chest pains were getting worse. There were moments when I felt short-winded for no reason. I constantly felt like I was having a bad asthma attack. My nervous energy made me spit on the sidewalk spontaneously for no reason.

My life seemed like something out of a bad science fiction or futuristic movie set in a parallel universe. Sometimes I had a hard time believing that all of this was actually happening to me as I slipped between consciousness and reality. Sometimes today I have a hard time believing that I lived that way for so long. If it weren't for the others who shared in my crazy life, I'm not sure I would believe it.

For example, on one particularly frigid night in Calgary, Canada, my friend Lorenzo and I trekked through the bitter cold. The whipping wind felt like bees stinging me all over my body. The temperature was below zero, and my fingers started to turn a bluish color and my toes became numb from the loss of circulation. All night long, we wandered the frigid streets of Calgary without a purpose or plan about where we'd sleep for the night, or how we'd survive.

Lorenzo and I were together after one of those you-can't-make-this-up chance encounters. Our roots go way back. We went to Visitation Valley Middle School and Jefferson High School together back in San Francisco, even playing together on Jefferson's state championship basketball team. We reunited in Calgary in 1993—just a few years out of high school—traipsing up and down the frosty streets of Calgary, 1,300 miles from home. I was in Calgary running for my life, while he was fleeing the inner-city streets of San Francisco, looking for better opportunities for his acting career. I was twenty-two, and he was twenty-one. And while our reasons for being in Calgary were extremely different, we shared our unsure and bleak-seeming futures.

When we first arrived in Calgary, we had no clue what the city had in store for us. I was willing to do whatever it took to stay free from the yoke of the Feds, but my money was getting tight and I was quickly running out of options. Although I was still able to survive, pay my bills, and take care of my personal needs, my situation was becoming more precarious by the day. I was looking to get into any type of criminal activity or racket that I could while living in Canada.

I had money saved, but my sole source of income at the time was periodic cash payments from a drug operation in Hawaii. But consulting fees are not the same as dealing direct and receiving the proceeds and profits firsthand, and I didn't want to get a money laundering case for having huge sums of money sent to me in Canada through a bank transfer or Western Union. So my options were limited.

As far as illicit activity and crime go, Canada was a slower-paced environment than I was used to. To a certain degree, I was a bit more street sharp than some of the natives, so there seemed to be an excellent opportunity to exploit the criminal marketplace. I could bounce between Vancouver and Calgary, moving unexpectedly from place to place as I had done my whole career. In the streets we called that "stick and move," a term straight out of boxing. However, I still had to be cautious. Although I was in another country, I couldn't afford to rack up any new charges or have a run-in with the law.

In addition, there were several barriers to entry into the drug trade that prevented me from jumping in with two feet to any of the illegal rackets. Existing criminal networks and well-organized gangs were protective of their territory and connections. The Hell's Angels had a very visible presence in Canada, particularly in Vancouver, which is the city I considered home base. At concerts and certain events, they would walk the streets in rowdy, impenetrable packs with vicious Rottweilers and baseball bats, clearly making it known that this was there territory.

There were also powerful Russian, Chinese, and East Asian networks that were organized and sophisticated with a predatory penchant for violence and eliminating the opposition. Singlehandedly, I was no match for any of these organizations. They could have smashed me like a fly on the wall. I was at a distinct disadvantage and completely out of my element. To do anything, I would have to move silently and stay under the radar.

Although Vancouver was home base, I would periodically pick up and go to other cities or provinces to hide out. Edmonton was always a good place to lay low. Although temperatures in the winter were regularly below zero, it offered a place of refuge when I wanted to get away. I knew the chances of the U.S. authorities coming to search for me deep in the interior of Canada were slim. My fugitive run in Canada, however, did include several close calls.

> My friend Ian and I are making the three-hour drive from Calgary to Edmonton. As we head down the Queen Elizabeth Highway, we joke and tell war stories about past criminal adventures. I notice that Ian is speeding. I humbly tell him to slow down, as neither of us could afford to get pulled over by the Royal Canadian Mounted Police (RCMP). He brushes me off. Within seconds, I'm

blinded by bright blue and red strobe lights.

"Damn!" I say aloud. *Life in prison,* I think silently. My mind starts frantically racing as I mentally rehearse what to say to the police if questioned.

Ian, who is AWOL from his parole officer in Washington state, is shaking like a leaf. I know his background, but he doesn't know mine. As I watch the police exit their vehicle in my rearview mirror, I have a sudden urge to burst out of the car to make a break for it. But we are in the middle of nowhere, and all I can see for miles are open fields. I wouldn't make it ten yards before being caught or possibly shot in the back. So I sit and anxiously fidget and fumble with my seatbelt as I try to discreetly wipe the sweat from my brow.

Time moves unbearably slowly as the officer walks to the car, suspiciously staring inside the vehicle, his right hand anxiously clutching his pistol holster. "Step outside the car please, sir." Before I know it, Ian is in handcuffs and being shoved headfirst into the backseat of the police car.

Common sense says I'm next. Two more unmarked police cars appear as if out of thin air and swerve to the side of the highway. The occupants are in plain clothes and look like the Feds. They cautiously walk to my window, tap on the glass, and tell me to step out of the car. They place me in the backseat of a separate vehicle and begin an intense cross-examination.

I'm on the hot seat while two Canadian federal agents blitz me with questions. The roadside interrogation lasts for about an hour, but I keep my composure and am able to stall them for a while. I'm pretty sure the Feds know I'm being deceitful; they probably recognize my nervous twitch, but they can't prove anything.

If we can't verify your identity, they threaten, we're going to take you straight to the immigration office and run your fingerprints.

Out of desperation, I give them two people to call to help me stall for time. One contact is in Edmonton and the other is my girl back home in San Francisco. This is a tricky prospect, but I know I can trust her instincts in dealing with the police—even though she has no idea what's going on or what alias I'm using. I have to take this chance, even though I'm pretty sure her phone is being monitored by the Feds. I had no other choice. I was desperate.

The gamble pays off. They release me—but only after I agree to report to the immigration office tomorrow morning to have my ID and background checked. I vow I will show up, but my plan is to immediately disappear into thin air. If I get out of this, I think, I'm going to go far away—someplace like Cuba or Europe where it will be harder for them to find me.

I call my girl later at a pay phone in San Francisco to get a report of what was going on. She told me that a Canadian federal agent had already called her house, hounding her repeatedly all morning. The agent was threatening her with federal prosecution and withholding information if she didn't cooperate and reveal my true identity. He demanded that she contact me and advise me to turn myself into the immigration authorities, but she didn't crack. Eventually the agent stopped calling, and I kept running.

That same day, Lorenzo frantically called me and told me the

Feds had come by his job in force with several agents, quizzing him about me. During my roadside interrogation, I had told them I was employed at Lorenzo's body-building gym in downtown Vancouver. It was the only verifiable thing I could tell them that could possibly persuade them to let me go. It was a calculated risk that backfired, though, because they wasted no time following up on that information. To add insult to injury, my apartment in Vancouver was right around the corner from the gym. The heat was on.

After the near disaster with the RCMP on the side of the highway, I felt like the walls were caving in on me and my money was evaporating like morning mist. It seemed like running was getting more expensive by the day. Although I didn't have children at the time, I had a younger sister whom I loved and cared for like a daughter, and I was helping my mother put her through St. Ignatius college prep, an exclusive private school back home in San Francisco. I had to quickly go to my playbook and come up with a plan, but my first order of business was staying free from the RCMP.

Now, the Feds in the United States *and* Canada were hot on my scent like bloodhounds. Although both countries offer plenty of places to hide across their vast land masses, I felt trapped. After the incident on the side of the highway, I decided to take a vacation of sorts. I boarded a private boat to Victoria, British Columbia, a quaint and quiet town on Vancouver Island with a small population. I stayed there for a while, then decided to keep moving—heading for Nanaimo, another small, sparsely populated town on the island. I needed time to think. I drifted back and forth between Victoria and Nanaimo for a while, getting myself refocused. While on the island, I tried to relax and be normal—tried to live the life of a square, average Joe. In the mornings, I would take casual strolls through the town and engage in casual conversations with the local townsfolk about the slow pace and the seclusion of small-town life. It was a humbling and peaceful experience, but my thoughts were constantly preoccupied with my life on the run.

After about a month, I returned to Vancouver, and I was more on point. Every move I made was well thought-out. A simple trip to the grocery store or gas station required precise planning.

I felt like I was being hunted and stalked like prey in the wild jungle. In this case, the FBI and the Canadian authorities were the predators. The emotional roller coaster ride was becoming bumpier and more turbulent. Every day, I felt a powerful combination of many emotions, and distrust and suspicion were always on the list.

Being in Vancouver had started to become nerve-racking. I couldn't freely walk downtown for fear of being stopped by the police. Although I trusted Lorenzo and he was my only real friend there, I had to be careful in my dealings with him, just in case the Feds were trailing him to get to me.

I vowed that I would never go back to the United States, even though my mind was already in the penitentiary. I swore that I would never turn myself in. They would have to kill me or catch me.

Eventually, though, it got too hot for me in Canada as well, with the authorities searching for me high and low in Calgary, Vancouver, and Edmonton. When I felt I had no choice, I would slip back and forth across the border, knowing any hint of a wrong move on either side could end this gut-wrenching game of cat and mouse.

10
THE POWER OF CONDITIONING

Frustrations, fears, and failures. Emotional roller coaster rides. Swinging back and forth on the brink of the breaking point. Spiritual holy war. Persistent pressure that could burst a pipe. Tapping into my deepest emotions. Getting in tune with all five senses. Thoughts of self-doubt and uncertainty about my future. The steady whisper of negative self-talk.

Given the loneliness and isolation of being on the run, I felt—and still sometimes feel—completely alone in the world. Even in my despair, however, I vigorously pledged to never self-medicate or deaden myself with drugs or alcohol, or to numb my mind with meds to mitigate the misery. I did and still do soberly confront my reality face to face.

In the absence of drug- or alcohol-induced suppression of emotions, my mind has sometimes been overtaken with confusion and chaos. The alienation and remoteness of being a Black man in society is enough to deal with; I had also been permanently branded as a fugitive and a felon. To some, this branding signifies the kiss of death.

I take full personal responsibility for my actions; however, there are certain circumstances that constructed the foundation of a framework that marginalizes Black men in this society and typecasts them as good for nothing. This foundation and framework often create a self-fulfilling prophecy.

Television, radio, and the Internet constantly bombard us with negative images and representation. In news and entertainment, Black males have most often been portrayed as vicious, gun-toting gangbangers—"super predators." In D. W. Griffith's movie *The Birth of a Nation,* released in 1915, Black men were portrayed as lustful rapists. Eighty years later, Hillary Clinton craftily and controversially alluded to the "super predator" portrayals in a speech in 1996 in New Hampshire. Today, we continue to be consistently represented as lyrically irresponsible rappers with our pants sagging to the ground or convicts in prison.

Rarely are we portrayed with positive images. As a byproduct of being given a negative image of myself at an early age, I was subliminally seduced into accepting these representations—and then I unintentionally supported and strengthened this negative imagery through my actions. Ultimately, I was a co-conspirator in my own downfall. The culture and messaging around me were my partners in crime.

Overwhelmingly negative images have the power to seep into the consciousness of society. Unbeknownst to many who are affected by this subtle and sly persuasion, this indirect programming often directs the most demeaning imagery at Black males. All kinds of people—Black males and otherwise—internalize the media message, which eventually leads to ugly statistics and negative side effects. Most notably, Black males make up only 6.5 percent of the total U.S. populace but over 60 percent of the prison and jail population. These statistics are particularly revealing.

My mixed emotions and discouragement about my country and my decisions to consciously rebel in the form of criminality started when I was a teenager who felt alienated and discriminated against in the world. Although I may not have been able to clearly express my thoughts and opinions about the system at a young age, I was blessed to instinctively and intuitively understand the world and how certain things worked; my perception of the world was that I was powerless within it.

Rarely did I see Black men in positions of power, such as in politics, heading major corporations—or companies of any size, for that matter—or in charge of anything that I could be proud of or would want to aspire to. The only "successful" Black folks that I saw were athletes and entertainers or dope dealers and hustlers. And even in athletics and entertainment, we were never the owners of teams or production companies. Something just didn't feel right about that.

I don't recall seeing any Black firefighters, and we had only one Black police officer in my neighborhood. I never once had a Black male teacher—someone who might have been better able to identify with my struggle as a Black boy. And if my memory serves me correctly, I only had two Black female teachers all the way up to the community college level. Not seeing Black adults in any position of legitimate or positive power does something to the mind and ultimately affects self-esteem.

The gangbanger and the dope dealer are often impacted by these patterns. They may be on the corner, but they are more observant and much more insightful and intelligent than people tend to give them credit for. Many of them—myself included—understand how the world perceives us. It's a plainly seen and felt perception. It's evident when we are repeatedly racially profiled, stereotyped, disproportionately imprisoned, and stopped and frisked for no reason—whether we have criminal records or not.

Over the years, as I became an avid reader and a serious student of history, my feelings of despair were intensified; often I would go into deep thought about the founding of this nation. There were fifty-six signers of the Declaration of Independence and thirty-nine signers of the Constitution, signed in 1776 and 1787 respectively. Both documents make up the indisputable foundation of the United States of America. At both historic events and in both historic documents, Blacks were visibly absent. Even worse, many of the men signing those documents actually owned slaves.

Unfortunately the leadership of today's major corporations, federal and state governments, and other major organizations look a lot like the men at those historic signings. Who leads today's powerful institutions? Predominately White men. Black men wield little political or economic power in the big picture of American society or on the world stage. This obvious lack of power can have demoralizing effects on the mind—especially for young Blacks in the inner city, many of whom feel they have nothing to live for in the first place.

As a young man, my negative self-esteem expressed itself in many different ways. One side effect of this low self-esteem translated into me being a manipulative womanizer. I found it was easier and more feasible to exercise control and power over a woman than to establish any position of authority over a corporation or government. I saw it as impossible to become a politician with power or a person who could change society and better the conditions of poor Black folks in my community or the world. I understood that the government didn't have control over my male body parts, so although I felt powerless in society, at least I could have all the sex I wanted.

Being susceptible and prone to violence is also a negative by-product of low self-esteem. It's easier to kill, shoot, or prey on someone on your block or in your neighborhood who looks like your seemingly impotent and worthless image than to exact war on something outside of your immediate world. Unfortunately, many Black kids and teenagers have been brainwashed to believe that killing another Black is trivial and meaningless; maybe in part because they also understand that killing a White person is likely to bring a stiffer consequence. Irony.

As human beings we have immense power within ourselves; God has given us power to control our minds and our thoughts, and we have self-rule over our actions. But realistically, from a global viewpoint—from a perspective of controlling resources in our communities, controlling the education of our children, and controlling capital and assets in the business world and corporate America—growing up as a Black boy and teenager, my reality did not reflect the God-given power of self-rule.

These are the roots that lead many of us to engage in a whole range of unproductive and damaging behaviors, selling drugs among them. We mistakenly think that we can control our own destinies by dealing dope. Contrary to popular opinion, many drug dealers don't have a high image of themselves and only feel validated when they have money or material possessions. At one time, I too fit this mold. I sought validation from society rather than self. I wrongly felt that money made the man.

Through custom and culture, Black men—including myself—have traditionally masked our true emotions and feelings about the world. We have been socialized to camouflage our vulnerability and insecurities by constantly demonstrating our masculinity with a hardcore façade. Often, this "masking" comes in harmful forms.

Although God gives us the will to choose, we are all heavily influenced by the cultures and communities that surround us. The phrase "becoming a product of your environment" is not a cliché; it is real. My parents were not investment bankers or doctors. I did not come from a so-called "good" family by society's standards, in terms of private schools, formal education, or rich and wealthy family members. I wasn't the beneficiary of a multimillion-dollar inheritance or trust fund handed down through generational wealth; neither were any of my friends in my community. Statistically speaking, the likelihood was low that I would become a corporate lawyer or congressman. Before anyone judges me or others "like me," they must also look at their upbringing and environment and circumstances they were born into. Those born wealthy in this country tend to remain wealthy, while those born poor tend to remain poor.

Black American men don't often share about our collective or individual relationships to society, and many of us hide our emotions, sometimes because we are too proud and don't want to show any sign of weakness, and sometimes because we simply do not have the language to articulate it.

I personally have nothing to hide. I am a mortal man. Man hurts. He feels. He cries. He fears. Men are sensitive but don't always make it apparent. We hide our emotions well. We conceal them underneath tough-looking tattoos, big muscles, menacing faces, and hardcore nicknames like "Capone," but many of us walk around society on eggshells or in a silent rage, harboring feelings of resentment.

In the words of James Baldwin, "To be a Negro in this country and to be relatively conscious is to be in a rage almost all the time."

11
INSATIABLE AND UNTOUCHABLE

As the unmarked police car creeps up beside me at the stoplight, I don't flinch. On the backseat is a huge duffel bag stuffed with enough drugs to get a life sentence, but I don't panic.

I'm not sure if it's nervousness or arrogance that prompts me to glance over my shoulder at the car next to me. I momentarily make eye contact with the occupants, then inch away slowly into traffic. As I pull away, I sip my grape juice and tighten my seat belt.

A lot of people would be spooked, but I am entranced by the money I might make from the next deal. I'm too hypnotized by the powerful potion of greed and arrogance to be scared.

I am driving a basic-looking rental car in Lake Minnetonka, Minnesota, a small, somewhat rural, upper-middle-class suburb near Minneapolis—99 percent White. Not too surprisingly, Black men are highly noticeable here among the hicks in the backwoods, sticking out like NBA players in the grocery store.

The police seem to follow me for a few blocks. I make a right and continue straight. Strangely, my nerves are calm and composed, but I know that if they continue to follow me, I will punch the gas pedal and take them on a high-speed chase through the streets of Hennepin County. I will not peacefully pull over; that is against my rules when riding dirty. I am already a fugitive from the Feds with a lot on the line, so I have a daredevil, do-or-die attitude.

Fortunately, after a few blocks, the car stops trailing me. It suddenly disappears from my rearview mirror. I continue to my destination, do the deal, and casually return home.

When I remember that scene, it seems like something out of an HBO movie that I watched instead of an event that happened to me. Oddly, the potential consequence of getting pulled over by the police, getting my cover blown, and possibly getting a life sentence didn't scare me the way it should have. I should have had the sudden urge to pee on myself, but the combination of arrogance and apathy I had developed from being a fugitive for years had left me disconnected from reality. I constantly drifted in and out of intentions and emotions. One minute I was careful and cautious; the next I was daring and adventurous. My common sense told me to be wary and try to avoid a life sentence, but ego and false pride sometimes trumped my intellect.

Over time, being a drug dealer had severely compromised my natural values and belief system. It made me conceited and cocky, and prompted me to act against good reason and behave irrationally at times. There were things I knew that I shouldn't do; I did them anyway. I knew many of my actions were dangerous to me mentally, spiritually, and physically, but I continued to do them.

In my soul, however, something just didn't feel right. My mother and grandmother instilled good values in me when I was a boy. I knew when to say *thank you,* and I respected older folks. I knew how to be humble and polite. As a child, I was like most children. I said, "Can I please . . ." and, "yes, ma'am," or, "yes, sir." But selling drugs was like declaring a spiritual jihad—a war with myself.

As I got older, I recognized the decline in my principles. As I drifted in and out of sleep every night, something would always internally pinch my spirit. It was a constant battle. I knew that it was wrong to prey on the weak, such as those with drug addictions. I was always uncomfortable when I entertained violent and sinister thoughts about physically hurting or maybe even murdering someone over something as petty as a $10,000 drug debt. Or when I plotted to lie in wait in the bushes for an unsuspecting enemy as they emptied the trash in the middle of the night in their pajamas.

Many days I dangerously hung on the cliff of becoming a coldhearted cutthroat. Where did I go wrong? When did I become obsessed with the fascination of money and power? For me, it was always a battle of Image versus Self—Malik the drug dealer versus Malik the man.

Malik the man is a quiet and laid-back bookworm with a heavy dose of inner nerd who is naturally nonviolent, loves to listen to Bob Marley or jazz legend John Coltrane, and enjoys quiet walks in the woods. Malik the drug dealer is a greedy, self-centered manipulator, only concerned with making the next deal. The double consciousness made me a walking contradiction.

I often wonder if other drug dealers are the same. Do they have a dual awareness as well, flipping and flopping and swaying in and out of touch with their own conscience? Do they turn their moral compass off and on as I have done in the past? Contrary to popular belief, many drug dealers have at least a basic concept of values and ethics and even spirituality; many drug dealers, gang members, and even killers believe in God or a higher power, too.

I was blindsided by the person I turned into when I pursued dealing—by my sudden lack of compliance to the moral code that lay dormant inside me. My ethical erosion happened slowly over time. It was like an innocent virus that festered and worsened into something malignant. Greed and arrogance infected and stained my spirit.

Selling drugs itself is a sort of a neurosis; it's an obsession that gradually takes control of the mind and behavior. Maybe that is why most drug dealers drink or use drugs themselves: in order to cope. Over time a mental mutation takes place. As time goes by, while they are anesthetized and numbed by a negative environment and circumstances, their moral code slowly subsides. Growing up, I sat back and watched many of my childhood friends make similar negative transformations.

Many guys that I grew up with started off playing Legos and video games; we clowned around in the middle of the street, played flag football, and went trick-or-treating like the rest of the kids in the neighborhood. However, as we grew older, some changed like I did, and some completely transformed, becoming murder machines, callous-hearted convicts, and beasts in human form.

Who could have predicted it? Could a third-grade history teacher predict that little Johnny with the big ears would grow up to be a murderous madman like Charles Manson or a drug kingpin like Pablo Escobar? Did the youth league football coach envision his ten-year-old star running back becoming an infamous criminal or gang leader? Did Grandma foresee her sweet and chubby-cheeked grandson later terrorizing other grandmothers, making them afraid of catching a bullet if they walked to the grocery store or stood at the bus stop?

Selling drugs severely compromises values on the individual level and also the principles and the integrity of an entire neighborhood. It totally destroys the community and its value systems. It breaks down and dissolves the family structure. It makes strong and powerful fathers become weak and feeble. It dishonors family matriarchs, many times turning them into unfit parents.

On one occasion, I bought a young lady's food stamps for pennies on the dollar—food stamps that were meant to buy food for her hungry children. I gave her drugs for the stamps, knowing that her children would go hungry. Although I was a teenager at the time, the greed and arrogance had already completely transformed me. On another occasion, I bought a man's wife's wedding ring for $20. Did I not understand the huge significance of disrespecting and completely disregarding that couple's precious and cherished nuptials and wedding vows? His wife was shattered when she noticed that her wedding ring was missing. In this particular instance, I'm happy to say, my conscience eventually kicked in and I gave the ring back free of charge.

There is no justification for my actions. But in the past, I have asked myself, were there systemic factors that helped me to make destructive decisions? When does it end? How many more kids have to go hungry because their mom sold their food stamps or the lunch meat from their refrigerator? How many women have to sell their bodies to get a hit? Would I and others like me do anything for a dollar? Must there be bloodshed for me to wear blood diamonds?

Charity and humility are the opposite of greed and arrogance. As I evolved from a normal kid playing kickball in the schoolyard at Panorama Elementary School to a nationwide drug dealer, my values flip-flopped. As a kid, I naturally shared my bag of Doritos or my Snickers candy bar with the other kids. Over time, however, I became a complete narcissist, a selfish individual with minimal empathy for others.

Like many drug dealers and criminals, I believe that my greed and arrogance were a direct result of unmet needs from childhood. I fallaciously thought selling dope would meet those needs. In prison I met hundreds of guys who had lost their flashy cars and expensive clothes and jewelry. Without their material possessions, they were no longer pretentious and proud; they were as shy as small children, timid and unsure of themselves.

The Bible says, "The love of money is the root of all evil," (1. Tim. 6:10), but this phrase doesn't tell the entire story: vanity, pride, and narcissism play a huge role as well. Many of these problems are also mentioned in "the Good Book," which specifically says, "Pride comes before a fall" (Prov. 16:18). I would find this out firsthand later in life.

Although my puffed-up pride and coldness to my fellow man may not have been noticeable with a cursory glance, and although my outward physical appearance was that of a normal human being, in actuality I was a beast in human form. I lived on the lower plane of existence as a reprobate who practiced premeditated sin. I was a walking contradiction, with a neat and unassuming look, and a predatory behavior that was based more on mental manipulation than violent actions. I projected myself as the smooth drug dealer, but my thinking was truly Machiavellian.

Many days I would dress low-key, sometimes resembling a college student with my Stanford University hoodie. This too was condescending; I thought people weren't smart enough to realize that I was an actual wolf in sheep's clothing.

Although I was already a fugitive from the Feds, greed compelled me to continuously risk life and limb—and perhaps a second life sentence—in order to relentlessly pursue the lure of money and the power that came with it. Why would I continue to flout the Feds and flaunt my fugitive status by continuing to sell drugs? I had known for several years there was an ongoing investigation and federal indictment, but I continued with my dirty dealing: a picture of arrogance.

Why did I continuously gamble with my life when I didn't necessarily need the money? I already had money put away. What compelled me to fly to Las Vegas on multiple occasions and gamble away thousands at the craps table? The potent combination of avarice and arrogance had intoxicated me, as it does for many. While some dealers initially sell as a means of pure survival or to feed their children, many continue to sell because of greed and gluttony.

Many dealers find their way to dealing through drug use, but my situation was different than most of my peers because I had never used drugs. However, we shared the same common denominator: greed. I didn't sell drugs to maintain a drug habit; it was strictly because of my initial need and subsequent unquenchable desire for money and power.

When I was coming up, the principles of greed and arrogance were preached and promoted by the OGs (older guys) in the neighborhood. Their messaging was and is clear: Make money no matter who you have to manipulate or take advantage of. This is evident in their actions when guys, young and old, uncaringly stand in front of someone's home or business and "do what they gotta do," displaying blatant disregard for anybody and everybody.

This set of principles is in no way exclusive to my community. It's the same in areas all across the country—White, Asian, and Latino communities included. Greed and arrogance are two common denominators for most criminals. Some can never get enough money or power, while others are arrogant enough to think we can forever outsmart the system.

The same attributes could be used to describe corporate and financial tycoons across the country as well; criminals and corporate hustlers may be different only in the eyes of the law.

'12
ART OF THE DEAL

In 1998 I was living in an exclusive condominium building called the Marquette Place in downtown Minneapolis. Other than a couple of NBA players, I was virtually the only Black person living in my building. Occasionally, I would see Minnesota Timberwolves point guard Stephon Marbury in the lobby or in the elevator and we would reluctantly—and maybe with a touch of arrogance and indifference—speak to each other. At the time I drove a rental car, a 1998 Dodge Intrepid. Something low-key and forgettable. When I introduced myself to people, I always used an alias; Dominique was the name I used most frequently.

I had been on the run from the Feds for five years; being cautious and observant had become part of my DNA.

While living on the run, I needed all the cash that I could get. So, over and over again I would reluctantly toss aside some of my caution and take risks so I could make money to survive. It seemed like $10,000 cash bundles disappeared into thin air like cigarette smoke. I had bills to pay in California, Seattle, and Minneapolis. But slowly, I would save up some sizable cash reserves that would last me a couple of years or so at a time by doing what I had done most of my adult life: selling drugs.

Transporting drugs from state to state while on the run was a logistical nightmare. I couldn't coordinate things or travel the way I wanted or needed to. All forms of public transportation were risky for me. The airports were an obvious security hazard—too many customs and DEA agents. I didn't trust the Greyhound bus or the train. Many times I had to trust my old drug connections to coordinate the deals and make things happen for me.

The challenges didn't end once I set things up on my end and received the drugs, especially if I was in a new state. Who would I market and sell my product to? Using my street savvy personality and networking ability, I developed a network of local dealers. These guys were transplants from Chicago and Detroit who had decided to manipulate the Minneapolis drug market. They were attracted to my no-nonsense yet laid-back way of doing business, which was a by-product of my always-suspicious but safe-as-possible way of operating.

One of my safety signatures included doing counter-surveillance and conducting a quick scan of my surroundings before leaving any location. Just before leaving any building, I would always walk around the perimeter to look for any suspicious activity. One can never be too careful.

I'm headed for a drug transaction so large that I know it could be my last deal. In the next hour or so, I could be dead or facing a second life sentence in prison. As I leave the building, I swiftly scan both sides of the street. I see nothing there, but I notice that the sky looks weird and has an eerie tint. *Is this a bad sign?*

I quickly get into my car and drive off. I circle the block twice. I make a left, then bust a U-turn. I pull over, park, and wait a few seconds. I drive off slowly. This time, there is no one trailing me.

As I head for my destination, questions float through my wandering mind. *Is this a set-up with the Feds? Is this a robbery attempt? Is this a hit on my life?* For a split second, I second-guess myself. *Maybe I should cancel?* Then I get a swift head rush: *Go!*

As I get closer to the destination, my phone rings.

"Hello?"

"Hey it's me. I'll be there in a few minutes. I'll meet you at the R . . . ."

Click. I hang up.

I sense that the guy on the other end was about to be reckless and irresponsible. If either of our phones are tapped (and I found out later that mine was), he would have been giving the Feds our exact meeting location.

I had met the guy on the other end of the phone call earlier in the day to discuss our pending transaction and the rules of engagement. We set the terms for the deal and agreed on a price. I gave very specific instructions to him and his crew: they would pay $200,000 in cash for my product. I made it clear how I wanted the money. No tens, fives, or one-dollar bills. I wanted the money neat and properly packaged in stacks of $10,000 with rubber bands tightly wrapped around each stack with all bills facing up and going the same direction. I told them to have the money in a black duffel bag. And most importantly: don't bring any new faces.

I also quietly and respectfully put them on notice that I had personal files on them: pictures of them, their houses, and car license plate numbers. "My people," I said, had these files. If my personal safety or freedom was in jeopardy, there would be swift and brutal consequences.

It was implicitly understood that we were putting our lives in each other's hands. We both knew that if things got hectic or went haywire, it could end in a life sentence for both of us, or even worse: death.

Leaving that meeting, that familiar lethal combination of greed and arrogance quickly overpowered any thoughts I had of defaulting on the deal. In the back of my mind, I felt I had nothing to lose. I had no wife or children (although my daughter would be born that same year). All I had was a life sentence smugly and patiently waiting for me in federal prison.

The guy I am meeting is from Detroit, then the murder capital of the United States. Guys from Detroit have a reputation for murdering for sport. On the surface, my contact seemed stable and steady; however, $200,000 is a lot of money, and plenty of people have been killed for less. I must be on my toes.

Although he has purchased product from me many times, I don't trust him. I keep him off balance, guessing and wondering. I never let him become familiar with my routine. Whenever we meet, I constantly change meeting locations, phone numbers, and methods of operation.

To pull off a $200,000 deal, I must use a bit of deception, to stunt. I have to make myself appear more powerful than I actually am. So I try to make myself look like the boss of a criminal organization. It's a bluff that can backfire if not done well. It's all about swagger and confidence—defense mechanisms out of my personal playbook.

During our initial conversation I had kept a poker face. I didn't talk much. I said few words and stayed only a few minutes. I knew that my confident posture spoke volumes. My body language was strong and upright. I was alone, but I made them think I had an army of assassins on standby—silent killers who weren't in sight, but were present. My life depends on my ability to outwit them, on making them feel a bit of fear and apprehension about any trickery or skullduggery.

I arrive at the meeting place early so that I can plan my potential escape route. Snowy and icy Minneapolis streets will present a potential problem if I have to exit quickly. This could get interesting.

I circle the block a couple of times looking for suspicious activity such as unmarked police cars. I look for guys who are ducked down low in parked cars. I look for Crown Victorias, which is what Feds typically drive. I look for any sudden or shady movements by anyone in the area. I use my keen peripheral vision to try to spot people making shifty eye movements. I see nothing unusual.

Once my surveillance is complete, I park down the block from my meeting destination. Now I sit and I wait. Although it's dark outside and most people would have problems seeing, I tend to operate better at nighttime. Being a fugitive has helped me develop infrared-like vision. My senses are sensitive and sharp to the point that I feel I have extrasensory perception.

A truck suddenly pulls up beside me. I click on. It's a vehicle I've never seen before. The window rolls down, and I see Detroit T. We pretend to smile at each other.

He tells me to get in the car with him. *Shit.* This is where it gets real. I must think quickly. *What is the vibe? What is my gut telling me to do?* If I move too slowly, it could arouse suspicion. If I look unsure of myself and let him sense any fear or hesitation, I could end up a dead man. I quickly hop out of my car, pop my trunk, and retrieve the duffel bag.

When I jump in his truck, I realize someone is sitting in the backseat. *Damn. One to the back of the head?* We are in a dark and deserted alleyway at 11 p.m., no witness or pedestrian in sight. They could kill me and dump my body in the alley, and I could lay there for the rest of the night, in the freezing cold and filth until my body is discovered by hungry rats, homicide detectives, or both.

I grab my phone and fake a phone call to "my organization." I speak two words into the phone: "It's good." We exchange duffel bags, and I swiftly jump out of the truck and back into my own.

I breathe a heavy sigh of relief and drive out of the alley as I reach for the money bag. *Is this bag full of counterfeit money or rolls of newspaper disguised as cash? Is the entire $200,000 in the bag? Are the Feds videotaping this transaction? Will I make it out of the alley alive? Is there a tracking device in the money?*

I unzip the duffel bag. It's cash for sure, but is it the whole $200,000? I will know for sure in the next hour.

I swerve to get on the freeway, then I suddenly get back off. I feel confident that I am not being followed. My driving seems erratic, but I am under control. There is a method to my madness.

I get back to my building. As I always do, I circle the block several times, make a few U-turns, and ensure the coast is clear before I park. I finally get inside and sit down with the money. I have a money-counting machine, so it shouldn't take long. After an hour I am done. It's all here: $200,000 in cash. Done deal.

Just as I finish counting the money, my phone rings.

"Hello." It's Detroit T. "Everything is good, I like the product. When can we do it again?"

"I'll call you in a few days."

Decisions, decisions. . . .

The money in Minneapolis was sweet. However, Minneapolis was ultimately where it all would start to go very wrong.

13
FACE THE MUSIC

In exchange for its financial generosity, Minneapolis took my freedom. It was there I was busted for the last time, after seven years on the run. After an exhausting path from the arrest to my federal sentencing, I could finally hear the trumpets of Gabriel blowing loudly, signifying it was October 26, 2000, my Day of Judgment.

I had anxiously anticipated this day for nearly eight years but it still didn't seem real. However, I could honestly say that I was relieved my life on the run and my constant worries about my fate were coming to an end. My emotions scrambled, I was a walking contradiction. I straddled the fence between agitation and calmness, but knew the day promised to bring closure. By the end of day, I would likely be serving anywhere from fifteen years to life in federal prison.

My arrest after seven years on the run had come seven months earlier because I had gotten lazy and started calling landlines instead of insisting on cell phones and phone booths. Through a tap on my father's phone line, the Feds tracked me down to a condo I was renting in Minneapolis. On April 12, as I was preparing to go to the gym, two FBI agents and one U.S. marshal burst through the front door.

I am a dead man. Life in prison.

I had pled guilty my first day in court, basically throwing myself on the mercy of the court and putting my fate in the hands of Federal District Judge Alan Bloch. When I was arrested, I had assumed there would be new charges from Minnesota or some other state, but the only charge against me was the one from Pittsburgh, and the Feds had offered me a deal that would expose me to fifteen years to life. By the time I was arrested, my case was seven years old, my already convicted codefendants refused to testify against me, the government wasn't sure it could locate any other witnesses, and they didn't want to spend money going to trial. I was ready for whatever would happen next.

It's around 5:30 in the morning, pitch dark outside, snowing with howling winds. Although this is normal fall weather for Pittsburgh, the storm feels like a bad omen to me. I lie in my metal bunk in my cramped county jail cell, but my mind is uncontrollably racing. I flash back to an innocent little boy playing kickball at Bayshore Elementary School. I dream of walking with friends to the corner store; we steal a bag of barbecue potato chips and run down the street, laughing wildly. I reminisce about how we would chase girls into the boys' bathroom at school, trying to get a kiss.

Today, there will be no flag football games in the middle of the street, no fishing for tadpoles in the creek. Today, I grow up. I will be treated as a grown man who has committed grown-man crimes. I will be forced to accept responsibility for my choices and decisions I've made over the last twenty-nine years. Today, I start to write a new chapter in my life.

"Wade, report to the sally port," I hear.

Inmates in the county jail report to the sally port before they leave the housing unit to go to court. I've been here awaiting sentencing for seven months now.

As I walk toward the sally port, other inmates in the unit somberly stare at me. They silently nod their heads in an upward direction as if they are ashamed to look me directly in the face. They know that I am a condemned man and that one day they too will take "the walk."

My cellmate, a big brute of a man about six-four and over 300 pounds, nicknamed Big Miami, solemnly walks over to me and says, "Keep ya head up, dog. Stay strong." Knowledge, a Muslim Brother from New York, says, "May Allah bless you." I thank them both and walk out of the sally port into the hallway.

I see a young guy who goes by Philly mopping the hallway. "Hey Wade, you going to get sentenced today?"

"Yeah."

In a flat tone, he says, "Hold ya head, Brah. I just got sentenced today; they gave me life. I am only nineteen and I don't have any kids."

I act as if I don't hear him and keep walking; but his voice echoes in my head as I walk out of the building. As I get into the van for the ride to the courthouse, fear starts to set in. Fear of the unknown is one of the worst fears a man can experience.

The van ride from the county jail to the courthouse covers only a few short blocks, but it seems like a cross-country trip. In the back of my mind I can hear the ricochet from Philly: *They gave me life.* The thought brings a lump to my throat. I close my eyes and drift off into a daydream for a few minutes.

"Wade! Wade! Come on, get the hell off of the van!" As I start walking toward the courthouse, the U.S. marshal roars, "WADE! Move faster!"

I bark back, "Man these cuffs are tight on my ankles; I can't walk faster!"

It's freezing, and I don't have a coat, so I'm shaking like a leaf from the cold. Or maybe I am shaking at the thought of getting fifteen to life.

I am taken inside and locked in a barren, steel-caged holding cell. I lie down on a thick slab of concrete, close my eyes, and start to daydream about my future. I am startled by a voice from the cell next to me. "Hey, Brah, you getting sentenced today?"

In a low stern voice, I say, "Yeah."

"I got sentenced this morning; they gave me thirty years."

I listen, but I don't say much. I'm not in the mood to talk. My bowels start bubbling as he shares his sentence. I try to lie still and relax. Suddenly I hear keys loudly jangling.

"Wade! Come on! It's time see the judge."

As the U.S. marshals escort me to the courtroom, I feel as if I am being marched to the electric chair. The walk from the holding cell to the courtroom, though only a few feet, feels like the length of a football field. Other prisoners in the adjoining holding cells divert their eyes; they don't want to look me in the face. One says in a miserable grim tone, "I am praying for you." I thank him humbly.

I stumble past their cells, shackled from waist to

feet. *This is where it gets real.* I try to mentally brace myself and also relax. Doesn't work. As I get closer to the courtroom, my muscles become tense and rigid.

I feel intimidated as I enter the massive and cavernous courtroom. I see people whispering in soft tones, staring at me with condemnation and disdain. It's like walking into a cemetery at night: ghostly and creepy with dim lighting. It becomes eerily quiet, and I can hear myself breathing. It reminds me of a haunted house, occupied by the ghosts of the souls who had been sentenced to prison before me, with the judge and the prosecutor in the roles of goblins.

Judge Bloch perches atop the bench, scornfully peering down at me with a gavel in his right hand—like an ax he would use to symbolically decapitate me. For several seconds, he stares at me with a blank, unwavering expression. I divert my eyes from the judge and see the U.S. attorney glaring at me.

In an arrogant tone, the judge begins to speak: "Malik Wade, today is a good day for you. I could sentence you to a life sentence without the possibility of parole. However, since you accepted responsibility and pled guilty in timely fashion, I am only going to sentence you to 169 months in federal prison."

I frantically calculate the math on 169 months. It hits me like middle linebacker Ray Lewis: 169 months is fourteen years! My emotions are mixed, part relief that I finally get closure and part dread as I stare off into space and think about walking the plank for fourteen long years.

My lawyer and the U.S. attorney look at each other. My lawyer fakes frustration and disappointment while his opponent gloats. I feel like the butt of an inside joke.

The judge continues to speak. "Malik Wade, I hereby remand you to the custody of the Federal Bureau of Prisons."

Two U.S. marshals immediately grip me by both arms and take me back to the holding cell.

Riding back to the county jail, I pensively stare out the van window. I look at the skyscrapers in downtown Pittsburgh and wonder what the people in those buildings are doing. I would give anything to be on the other side of that window.

When I finally get back to the county jail, I sluggishly walk back to my housing unit. Some inmates are laughing, clowning around, playing cards and dominoes. When they see me, everyone sort of stops. I know from their facial expressions that they want badly to ask me what happened in court, but they say nothing.

I stay silent, walk straight to my cell, and shut the door. I flop down on my bunk and begin to visualize my new life. After a few minutes, I hear a knock on the door.

"What's up, Brooklyn?"

"How you doing, Brother Malik? You good, Brah?"

"Yeah, just getting my mind right."

"What happened at court today?"

"They gave me fourteen years."

"Damn, Brah."

"Yeah, I know. But it could have been life."

"You are strong; you can handle it."

"I know. Look at you, Brooklyn; you ain't never going home. You have life and you still have a smile on your face every day."

"Yeah, I can't let them take my personality from

me. Okay, Malik, I was just checking on you. If you need anything, let me know. I'm cooking my special Top Ramen noodle soufflé tonight with a side of Dorito chips. Want some?"

"No thank you, Brother, but thanks for asking."

We both smile and agree to talk later. I drift off to sleep. I wake up around 4 a.m. This is the first day of my new life. This is my first day as a convicted felon.

After enduring the cumbersome and time-consuming process of the federal court system for months since my arrest and weeks since my sentencing, I was mentally and emotionally fatigued and anxious to start serving my prison time. In the county jail, I felt like I was living in limbo. The miserable conditions of the county jail stifled me and made me edgy.

There were few—if any—resources that would help me better myself in the county jail: no college classes or programs. My access to books was limited because I was being confined to my cell pending transfer. I was allowed out only for one hour per day to exercise and take a shower. Ironically, I couldn't wait to get to prison.

In the middle of the night, I hear a loud knock on the door and some keys clanging. The door flies open. A bright light shines in my face.

"Wade! Wade! You are being transferred. Be packed and ready to go in ten minutes."

It's about 3 a.m., but I'm always on the ready for action while in prison, even while sleeping. I quickly get up and gather my personal property, including my legal paperwork, and I'm ready to go in seconds. When the correctional officer opens the door, I quickly run down the hall to say good-bye to a couple of guys.

Brooklyn is on his knees, praying, when I arrive at his cell. As he gets up and walks to the door, I tell him to stay strong and keep the faith. He looks at me sadly and doesn't say a word. As I back away from his cell door I can feel his pain. He struggles to find the right words, but ultimately says nothing. I bend down and slide a note under his cell door with my federal register number and full name, and tell him to stay in touch.

I turn around abruptly then run down the hallway to young Philly's cell. His light is on, and he is reading. I tell him I'm leaving and that I want him to hold his head up, stop watching so much TV, and get into the law library to continue to fight his life sentence. Like Brooklyn, Philly doesn't say a word. He looks at me, drops his head, lays back down on his bunk, and continues to read.

Even though they both appear to ignore me, I don't take it personally. I know it's a defense mechanism. Neither of them want to see me go. It happened so suddenly; I think they are both somewhat stunned. This is their way of saying good-bye to a dear friend. I slowly walk away without saying another word.

Our exchanging of good-byes is poignant and powerful, if not traditional. We know we will never see each other again, as Brooklyn and Philly are both serving life sentences.

"Wade! Wade! Hurry up! I don't have all damn day! Do you want to stay here with your buddies?"

"Okay! Okay!"

I pick up my bag with my books and personal belongings and vanish.

Obviously, prison is not the best place to make friends; lasting friendships in prison are rare. However, there are exceptions, and some prison friendships extend beyond the walls.

Usually, the relationships established in prison are dysfunctional—unhealthy and based on some form of manipulation. I rarely experienced real friendship in prison. Aside from the obvious common denominator of being in prison, there were very few guys in prison that I connected with mentally or spiritually. Many of us were the same in a lot of ways, particularly as it relates to our backgrounds and upbringing, but we were also very different. For the most part, I had very little personal interaction with over 90 percent of the inmate population.

But the need to have a good friend in prison is no different than the need for a good friend in society. A good friend in prison is someone you can talk to when you are feeling down and depressed; someone with whom you can share personal information and valued secrets; someone to discuss the problems you are having with your children, your wife, or girlfriend; someone to hear your insecurities, your fears, past mistakes, or future goals and dreams.

All human beings need healthy social interaction and mental stimulation. Guys in prison are no different. In fact, they are often in more desperate need than others because prisoners are more emotionally exposed and vulnerable.

Every prisoner is looking for something or someone to help numb their pain. They are looking for some sort of peace of mind or momentary relief from the constant pressure, the stress, and the suffocating boredom. For some, momentary relief comes in the form of a good friend who can tell a timely joke or happily reminisce about better days. When a prisoner calls home and receives bad news—such as the passing of a close relative— a good friend can offer temporary relief with a positive attitude and word of encouragement.

A good friend in prison may be someone you go to breakfast with every morning, someone you exercise with every day, or someone that you study the Bible or Quran with or pray with daily for years. A good friend may have a calming, reassuring influence that can prevent you from getting into trouble or becoming unnecessarily violent and volatile. And a good prison friend will also have your back if you do have to become violent and defend yourself in a confrontation.

Many men won't admit their need for a friend—they want to uphold an image of being invincible and macho. Appearing weak or emotionally needy is the ultimate taboo in prison. However, when you develop a genuine friendship with someone who is unexpectedly transferred or released, the shift can derail your focus and disrupt your normal routine.

When a dear friend leaves, it is a natural human instinct to miss their presence; it is the same in prison as in any other friendship or relationship in society. Eventually, however, you readjust, refocus, and move forward. When you develop a true friendship with someone in prison—despite its inability to change your circumstances—that friendship can change your life.

14
TRANSFER

"Wade, hurry up and get off of the van! You are getting on the airlift! You're going to Oklahoma!"

"What do you mean Oklahoma? I asked the judge to transfer me to a prison in California! I am calling my lawyer!"

"You can call President Bush if you want! But right now get the hell off the van!"

I defiantly exit the van that transported me from the Allegheny County Jail as the U.S. marshal snickers and glares at me.

It's snowing lightly as I wait in the gusty twenty-degree weather. Hundreds of federal prisoners are being herded onto a plane at a private landing strip near Pittsburgh. The secretive airstrip resembles a military blockade as marshals and other government guards patrol the perimeter with an arsenal of high-powered military weapons. The marshals running this federal prisoner exchange process are making sure no one attempts to escape.

Trying to board a plane with shackles around my waist, wrists, and ankles proves extremely difficult, especially because I am wearing a special device called the "black box." Because I was a wanted fugitive for seven years, I am considered an escape risk; therefore, it has been mandated that I be confined to the black box every time I am transferred.

The black box is made out of unbreakable thick plastic that covers the top of my handcuffs. The device looks simple and harmless but is unbearably painful, severely limiting my hand movement and preventing me from even wiggling my wrists. Every time I try to adjust my hands to ease the throbbing in my wrists, it feels as if the device grips my handcuffs even tighter. After several hours with the black box, my handcuffs start to slice into my flesh and cut off the circulation in my hands. Internally, I scream in agony. It feels like low-intensity torture.

As I board the plane, I am struck by a sharp stench of bitterness and hostility. As I shuffle to my seat, I can feel the eyes of the convicts who are already on the plane; it seems as if everyone on the plane is staring at me. I try to avoid eye contact while discreetly scanning the plane, searching for a familiar face to reduce my discomfort. What I see are threatening faces that are hard as concrete; many are entirely covered in tattoos or huge ugly scars—war wounds from prison fights and riots—and noticeable bruises and gashes. Everyone on the plane seems angry.

These prisoners have "the 1,000-yard stare," a blank and vacant look that signifies a defeated soul. They look shell-shocked and traumatized, like the life has been sucked out of them. I can only imagine what they are thinking. I know what I am thinking, though: *Damn, fourteen long years ahead.*

I will later learn that many of these prisoners are serving life sentences and have been in prison for ten, fifteen, twenty years or more. Most are tired and ready to give up. I'm surprised by the large number of women prisoners on the plane—partially separated from the men and seated in the front rows. I see White, Black, Native American, and Hispanic women. Some of them look tougher, harder, and more battered than the men.

As soon as I sit down, the guy next to me strikes up a conversation. I think he is talking out of nervousness and as a defense mechanism. His name is Sleepy, and he's a nineteen-year-old Hispanic guy from Texas. He tells me he has just been sentenced to thirty years for bank robbery and carjacking.

Over the next several hours, as the plane crisscrosses the United States, dropping off and picking up other prisoners, Sleepy tells me his life story as a validated gang member from the Texas Syndicate. He is worried that Hispanic gangs will prey on him once he arrives at his prison in Beaumont, Texas. Sleepy is unsure if he will have any friends or homeboys from his neighborhood who could help protect him at the prison. I tell him to be careful and observant of his surroundings. Who am I to judge or give useful advice? I am a rookie as far as prison goes. As Sleepy gets off the plane, he leans over and whispers, "I'm scared, homie."

Around 6 p.m. the plane finally lands in Oklahoma City. Everyone still on the plane looks weary and worn out. Some of us have been on the plane for seven to eight hours, cramped and confined in shackles that make it hard to move and nearly impossible to use the bathroom. I have had very little to eat since my 3 a.m. wake-up call at the Allegheny County Jail. They fed us on the plane twice. Both times the meal consisted of a small bottle of water, a rotten apple, a couple of crackers, and an old slice of cheese.

"Off the plane!" the marshal snaps. We wearily get out of our seats and slowly shuffle down the aisle. To my amazement, as I exit the plane, I never even touch free ground. I step right into the prison itself.

The Oklahoma Federal Prison Transfer Center houses federal prisoners who are being transferred to various prisons throughout the U.S. and the world. It confines a huge melting pot of prisoners from all ethnic backgrounds—Blacks, Hispanics, Whites, Native Americans, Europeans, Nigerians, Russians, Jamaicans, etc. Almost every U.S. state and city is represented.

Once inside the prison, my shackles were removed, and I was processed and evaluated by medical staff, a psychologist, and several other government employees. Then I was shoved into a cramped and cold holding cell made of cinderblock and concrete; dozens of us were packed in like sardines. The room felt like a powder keg of emotion that could explode into a full-scale riot at any second. Many of the guys were still in shock from receiving a life sentence earlier in the day. Some had been in prison for decades. Others were experiencing their first day in prison. The stress level was suffocating.

One of the most interesting and ironic things I noted about the Oklahoma Transfer Center experience was how freely information flowed between the prisoners. The prison grapevine seemed as efficient as the Internet itself. I sat back and watched intently as prisoners huddled up in small groups and exchanged cryptic mental and verbal notes and "kites," handwritten notes hidden in the orifices and cavities of the body such as the butt cheeks or under the scrotum sack or sometimes swallowed and released later.

They shared information as if their lives depended on it, enthusiastically discussing which prison just had a race riot, which prison was the most violent, who was getting out, who was coming in, who was a snitch, etc.

The white-collar criminals traded information on stock tips, then hurried to the phone and called their brokers. Others got tips from high-powered mob men who had connections on the outside, then called their bookies on the streets and placed bets on major sporting events.

Once processed into the prison and assigned to a housing unit, they would call family and friends to send messages and gossip, and share about who they had just run into in transit. In a split second, a shot could be called on the streets—good or bad—or a major decision could be made that could affect the entire prison population in the United States or an entire neighborhood or city.

The communication system was powerful beyond belief. Based on information received while in transit, prisoners could make things happen anywhere at any time. The government couldn't stop it. The correctional officers couldn't stop it. It was impossible to isolate hundreds—if not thousands—of prisoners who were transported and traded through this massive "human switchboard."

This experience was completely unique and could never be replicated because this was the only prison in the United States that had so many different prisoners from so many different places throughout the world. Also, the prisoners here were the most powerful prisoners in the world, such as the high-profile terrorist suspects charged with helping the 9/11 attacks, well-connected mob men like John Gotti, international drug traffickers and cartel members, and billionaire white-collar crooks like Bernie Madoff.

As a student of history, I compare the entire experience of the Oklahoma Federal Prison Transfer Center to what captured African slaves must have experienced in the fifteenth century, when the Spanish and Portuguese slave ships arrived on the west coast of Africa. The traders would capture members of various tribes, then take them to a central location that must have been similar to the Oklahoma Transfer Center where they would be divided up to be transported to the United States, the Caribbean, Brazil, etc.

En route, the slaves from these different tribes with a variety of languages and dialects would attempt to communicate with each other. They must have looked at each other with confusion and shock, trying to figure what was actually happening. The slaves' puzzled and panicky facial expressions are combined with intense stares and hard looks between the captives, a scene strikingly similar to the experience of the captured federal prisoner. This unspoken coded communication is such a powerful phenomenon that it cannot fully be put into words. It can only be felt or experienced firsthand.

15

FINDING MY WAY

Once I finally got to my designated prison, Taft Correctional Institution in Bakersfield, California, I had mixed emotions. In a sense, I was relieved and glad that running from the Feds was over. I was thankful that the court proceedings were done and that I was no longer living an unpredictable and unstable life. However, I was also seriously concerned and unsure about how things would play out over the next fourteen years.

My first day in prison shook up my entire central nervous system. The prison ecosystem creates its own very distinct sights, smells, and sensations that I had never experienced before: the sour stench of decades-old urine in the bathrooms, the creepy feeling of taking a shower among other men, the palpable tang of tension rising from gang members and opposing cliques. In addition, the rude, disrespectful and sometimes abusive behavior of the correctional officers sort of stunned me.

That first day can be described in three words: fear, embarrassment, and stress. It wasn't a physical fear of violence or of not being able to defend myself against would-be predators, but a fear of the unknown. I didn't know what situations I would face or how to react when I did. I wasn't sure if I should be humble and low-key or antagonistic and assertive.

When I first walked into my assigned housing unit, I could see menacing-looking men with mean mugs and frowning faces in every direction that I looked. They were hunched over and huddled in small groups, rubbernecking at me while whispering together. It felt like they were all conspiring against me and pointing at me with their noses. I instantly sensed negative vibes, and the tension that had begun when I walked in rose as we suspiciously eyeballed each other. I quickly realized that being humble was completely out the window. It could be viewed as a weakness. I would still be low-key but definitely more assertive.

When I first arrived, several correctional officers made me strip down, completely naked, as they roughly and rudely searched and examined me. They made me bend over and spread my butt cheeks open wide as they thoroughly inspected the inside of my rectal cavity with a flashlight, and studied and stared at my testicles, supposedly searching for drugs and weapons as I stood there humiliated with my manhood dangling before them—literally and metaphorically. I felt as if the officers took personal pleasure as they sadistically watched me reluctantly disrobe and obey their commands. This experience was downright demeaning and left me feeling completely humiliated. Prior to prison and jail, my naked body had never before been seen by another man. The thought made me absolutely furious.

Stress erupted from a blunt realization hitting me like a sock to the face: I would be stuck in prison for a very long time. There is very little sentence reduction for good behavior in federal prison, and federal inmates serve an average of 87 percent of their sentence.

That first day in prison changed my life forever.

After learning my way around and meeting a few people, I started to gradually develop a routine and slowly adjust to prison life. I decided to enroll in college and take some computer courses and business classes to engage my mind and help me avoid thinking about how much time I had to serve. I felt strongly that education would be the only thing that could save me.

Over time I started to learn some very valuable lessons from my prison experience, such as sacrifice, patience, and humility. I had to sacrifice time with some of my friends who continuously wanted to partake in criminal conduct inside the prison while retelling old war stories about past criminal misadventures and scandalous escapades. Some of the stories were as captivating as an HBO blockbuster, and I sometimes willingly participated in the tomfoolery and tall-tale telling, but deep down I *knew* I was engaging in foolishness and frivolity. And I knew I could not live this way for the next fourteen years.

During my prison incubation period, I also had to learn patience. I learned that it would not be easy to change my negative ways and unhealthy mind-set. It was hard to break habits such as using foul language and cursing every other word, and hard to stop being suspicious and cynical of everyone at all times and hard to not view everyone as my enemy. It was also difficult to shed my disrespectful tendencies and negative views toward women. However, over time, with patience, I eventually conquered most of my bad habits.

While in prison I had to learn discipline. I developed a routine of consistently studying every day at the same time, in the same place, regardless of distractions. It didn't matter if there was about to be a prison riot, a lockdown, a prison strike, or a Los Angeles Lakers playoff game featuring Kobe Bryant. It didn't matter what gossip a friend had to share about who just beat up who. I disciplined myself to stay steadfast and focused on my studies and self-improvement.

I tried to train my mind to think positive. Instead of being negative and pessimistic, like most of the prison population, I worked to develop a positive outlook. I tried consistently to do the right thing, to be humble and polite, consciously avoiding others who got into trouble and frequently went to "the hole." Discipline was a saving grace for me and has become a part of my DNA.

As my time in prison progressed, I became more insatiably hungry and thirsty—not for food and beverage, but hungry for things such as intellectual improvement, spiritual insight, and the desire to do better. I wanted to shed my old snakeskin and reveal a new version of myself. I wanted prison to be a cleansing and purification process. I wanted to rid myself of the impurities, toxicities, and multiple layers of contamination, cancers, and poison that were inside me—things that had manifested themselves in my mind, spirit, and body at different points throughout my life.

I wanted to dispel the myths and misunderstandings about men who go to prison. Prison motivated me to defeat the negative stereotypes and stigmas about Black men in society; it made me want to stun the nonbelievers and cynics who said, "You can't do it," and, "You'll be back." I wanted to disappoint the doubters who expected me to return to prison within three years of my release, as dictated to them by subjective data they had studied from the Bureau of Justice Statistics.

Prison is a matter of perspective. Prison can be a fertile ground for personal growth and development or a toxic wasteland. I believe that the worst experience in the hands of a wise man can be the cause of his own salvation. Even prison can be a good thing for some, despite the many mental and physical horrors it inflicts on its inmates. Many well-known individuals throughout history have gone to prison and later ended up having tremendous and enduring impact on society. The list includes Malcolm X, Nelson Mandela, Paul the Apostle, Martin Luther King Jr., Fyodor Dostoevsky, and Gandhi, to name a few.

There is much to debate and discuss about how prison experiences affected these men and ultimately their influence on the world. Through diligent reading and study, I have been able to vicariously share their experiences and apply many lessons and parallels to my own prison experience. In many respects, I feel we are kindred spirits. I identify with many of Malcolm X's philosophies, particularly a statement he makes in his autobiography: "I don't think anybody ever got more out of prison than I did.

"In fact, prison enabled me to study far more intensively than I would have if my life had gone differently and I had attended college in the more traditional manner. Where else but prison could I have attacked my ignorance by studying for fifteen hours a day?" I find Malcolm's statement profound and befitting.

Ultimately, prison was the epitome of cognitive dissonance, given its contrasts and contradictions. Prison shook my existing belief system to the core, but it was also the origin of my personal progression and my "Road to Damascus" moment. It opened my eyes and helped me evolve into a philosopher, someone who asks questions about the world around me. I began to personally ask questions about the meaning of life, as Job did in the Bible. For the first time, I asked myself questions such as, *Who are you?* and, *Why are you here on this earth?*

By the time I left prison, I had a clear understanding of the answers to these questions.

16
MENTAL WARFARE

Prison was more of a mental struggle for me than a physical one. I describe the reality of prison as low-intensity mental warfare; it's a mind game. More than a game, actually, prison is the ultimate mind-fuck. To survive prison, the mind must be able to withstand immense amounts of pressure. In federal prison particularly, where sentences often last for decades, the prisoner must make many mental adjustments to cope.

To survive you must be able to protect yourself from the covert and overt psychological attacks on your mind by prison authorities, who hound and harass, even when prisoners are fully complying with all rules and regulations. They use every possible tactic, trick, and technique to mentally and physically crush prisoners into submission—to force them into completely succumbing and surrendering their souls.

Although they had my body, I determined I would never give them my mind.

To persevere in prison, you cannot get discouraged upon experiencing failure or disappointment, even when you're denied basic rights like a shower, or a transfer to a prison closer to home, or a visit with family, or time to use the phone. Prisoners must learn to accept the reality of their situations while maintaining self-worth and sanity. The will to fight and survive must be nurtured. It's a nuanced and complex mental dance.

The prison environment is cancerous on multiple levels, but particularly in terms of how it affects interactions with others and general communication and social skills. For me, prison was not favorable to developing healthy social interactions. The rules of social engagement and etiquette in prison are strange and unconventional, and given the unnatural and toxic environment, most relationships are predestined to be abnormal or awkward.

At times, I felt my social and communication skills start to slip away. In addition, due to lack of healthy stimulation, I sometimes felt I was mentally regressing in my own development. My speaking and language skills, including my diction, became a lot less crisp and there were times I felt as if I was slurring my syllables. This was most severe during the times when I was in solitary confinement with very little human contact. Although there is no replacement for human touch or the mental stimulation that human contact can provide, I turned to reading or meditation and praying as substitutes in order to keep my mind sharp. Prison is the epitome of sensory deprivation and classical conditioning. Every day I prayed that I would not become desensitized and completely lose my footing, or become mentally programmed like Pavlov's dogs that slobbered and salivated whenever they heard a bell, as they had learned to associate bells with getting fed.

In prison, my body was technically under complete jurisdiction of the federal government. I had no way to prevent being physically trespassed against by the prison staff as even basic bodily functions such as using the bathroom could be controlled and manipulated. The prison influenced and controlled almost all physical stimuli, like scientists setting up a study or a lab test. I often felt like the subject in a control group experiment.

On several occasions I was abruptly transferred in the middle of the night to a different prison thousands of miles away without explanation or rationale. My relationships with people both inside and outside the prison were at the mercy of the administration. It was nearly impossible to maintain a healthy relationship with a woman on the outside, and I was given a very limited amount of phone time per month to call family and friends. My mail was censored. Visitors had to pass background checks, and my visits were closely monitored, making family and friends feel as if they were in prison themselves.

Because of the pressure and the difficulty in maintaining a connection with me, some family and friends gradually started to distance themselves and ultimately faded away. Letters became sporadic. Phone calls home turned into monologues—with me doing all of the talking—as my attempts to spark conversation proved awkward and ineffective. People just didn't want to be bothered. They had responsibilities and relationships, husbands, wives, children, jobs. They had barbecues, baby showers, and Super Bowl parties to attend. They wanted to attend to their duties, have fun, and live their lives without being burdened by someone calling from prison and dampening their day. Fortunately, I caught on quickly and stopped calling as much, concentrating instead on serving my time.

Being in prison is a horrible experience, but being in prison far away from home is the worst. Like a FedEx package, I wound up being shipped all over the United States to prisons and jails in ten different states. I stayed in some places for years, others for only a day. I was imprisoned in Minnesota, thousands of miles from family and friends, where the temperatures in winter often drop to ten degrees below zero. I was incarcerated in Colorado where I was surrounded by hundreds of miles of mountain ranges that stretched as far as the eye could see. I was confined in Oregon where the endless rain sapped all of my energy, making me feel moody and melancholy. Calling home to California from places in Pennsylvania, Indiana, Wisconsin, Oklahoma, and Georgia made me feel as if I were calling from the moon.

Losing control over my own body was a huge adjustment. Prior to prison, I would spontaneously travel at a moment's notice. On Monday I might be in Las Vegas shooting craps at Caesar's Palace. Tuesday I could be shopping in New York on Madison Avenue, and Friday eating in an upscale restaurant in the Georgetown area of Washington, D.C. In prison, however, I had nowhere to go. Some days I would walk the exercise track in the prison rec yard and just stop in my tracks, gazing at the double razor-wire fences that hemmed me in. The fences clearly signified that I was stuck!

On the outside, the more outspoken a person is, the more oppression he is likely to face from the authorities. It's not much different in prison: the more mentally strong and defiant a prisoner is, the more likely the prison staff will attack him. I resolved to be strategic in my outspokenness and rebellion. When situations arose, I always did a cost-benefit analysis before I bucked the system. I knew some battles just couldn't be won. As the proverb goes, "The art of being wise is knowing what to overlook."

However, there were battles that could be somewhat successfully waged, and I learned that in prison the pen is much mightier than the sword. Although the prison grievance policy is a bunch of red tape—time-consuming and incredibly tedious—it is the only available source of possible remedy. I became a master of the prison grievance process and the paperwork it required. Over the years, I helped countless fellow prisoners file paperwork to get proper medical care or a reinstatement of visiting or phone privileges. I even helped some guys get time knocked off of their original prison sentence.

Obviously, I knew I could not win a physical confrontation with the prison authorities; that is a fool's bet. With the heavy weight of the government behind them, they could have smashed me like a bug. They had high-powered guns, mace, and pepper spray, along with tactical goon squads and cell extraction teams. I have seen prison authorities subdue the biggest, toughest gang members and heard cold-blooded murderers cry out for mercy as they were being viciously beaten, kicked, and stomped by prison staff.

Witnessing such scenes made me realize that I had to be much more premeditated and deliberate. Did I want to get my teeth kicked in? Was I willing to get my head split open by a baton? Getting permanent scars from having my face bashed in would not be the moral victory that I wanted. Did I want to be able to brag about surviving beatings? Hell no!! I had to plan and be calculating so I could save face—literally and figuratively—without compromising my values. It was all part of a very specific plan to navigate the prison land mines and beat the system by employing the philosophy of martial arts—using the prison against itself.

I had to learn to control my internal anger. Although I have never been an outwardly volatile person, like any other human being, I too have a volcano just beneath the surface. This volcano nearly violently erupted one day as I was sitting in the prison sports television room watching a college basketball game. I loved college basketball, and it was one of a few things that could ease the pain of prison for me. Suddenly, a guy named Monster, a rough-and-ready Crips gang member, walked up and abruptly changed the channel without acknowledging me. Then, he turned and scowled at me defiantly. I instinctively jumped up to turn the channel. We squared off in our combat stances and stood nose to nose silently. I could smell the Doritos on his breath.

We stood there for what seemed like hours but was probably a few seconds. My thoughts raced. *Should I viciously strike first? What is he going to think if I let him get away with this shit? Is it worth it? Is this my TV? Do I really care? Do I really have to watch the game? Do I eventually want to go home to my family? Do I want to risk us potentially seriously injuring or maybe even stabbing each other over a government TV?* After quickly reviewing these questions in my mind, I chose to humble myself and bow out gracefully. I walked away but I cussed and fussed and spoke my mind. Then I went straight to the prison yard and did 1,000 push-ups to reduce my rage.

Despite temptations like this one, I never lost sight of my ultimate goal: to get out of prison and stay out. I did not care to stay in prison, to become a prison hero, or an OG (Original Gangster) or shot caller with war stories to tell. Prison is a miserable place. Although I learned a lot while there, I hated it.

I never met anyone in prison who was actually happy to be there. Although some develop a sense of closure and peace because they know they will never go home, they will never be *happy* to be in prison. Even the ones who have lost touch with reality or take psych medications to cope or sleep all day are unhappy about being in prison.

Even so, some prisoners are happy to cultivate a "reputation" in prison. But I knew that having a big reputation in prison meant nothing in the real world. I had a release date; I would be back in the real world one day, so I understood that having a rep in prison is complete bullshit of the highest order. To be known as a killer or have a reputation for being tough while someone else controls your entire life is the ultimate contradiction. How could a person consider himself a gangster or tough guy when somebody else controls all of his reality?

Of course, having a tough guy rep can offer a kind of protection against physical attacks and help keep a prisoner safer. Consequently, to a degree, I do understand why some prisoners choose this tactic. I chose instead to prevent and minimize the possibility of being physically confronted by staying in tip-top physical condition. In prison, size matters.

Although it was very difficult for me to humble myself and not engage in mortal combat over the TV, I chose to swallow my pride. This guy had a thirty-year sentence, was wretched and miserable, and had nothing to lose. From what I heard, he had done nothing but watch music videos and sports for the last fifteen years of his prison life. He was homicidal and probably suicidal. He was literally ready to kill or be killed over the TV. How could I win? I couldn't.

Yes, I would always defend myself and demand respect if in imminent danger, but I had bigger dreams beyond the prison walls. Because of this situation, I rarely watched television the last seven years of my prison sentence. It was all a part of my long-term strategy, part of the mental game I waged against prison.

In prison, as in the outside world, you have to be a strategic thinker.

17
TRUE EDUCATION

When I got to prison, I quickly learned that the prison itself would not educate or rehabilitate me. The staff and prison administration are not concerned with rehabilitation—only punishment. Any changes or improvements to better myself would have to come from my own initiative. Upon my arrival, I set two immediate goals:

1. Make a specific list of educational goals that I wanted to accomplish while incarcerated. These would include learning how to speak Spanish and Swahili, the native tongue of my ancestors; learning about the stock market; and learning how to sell real estate; and

2. Develop a comprehensive must-read book list. With a lot of years ahead of me and plenty of time to study, I felt I could make tremendous strides in my reading, my educational enhancement, and my overall development. I figured that if I read just one book per week (four per month), I would finish 672 books over fourteen years!

After that much reading, I thought, I should have a decent amount of knowledge and information under my belt that I could potentially use in the real world. I immediately started to ask other serious readers in the prison for their recommended readings. Their suggestions ranged from *The Autobiography of Malcom X* (my favorite) to Mark Twain's *Huckleberry Finn.*

Reading became my salvation and more. It became my emotional comforter and an analgesic to numb my pain. I used reading to escape the reality of my circumstances and to alter my state of consciousness. I had never used drugs or alcohol, but reading gave me a buzz—a natural high.

My learning experience in prison was transformative and life-changing on many levels. Most important to me was that my educational process was organic and natural; it came from within. I wasn't merely receiving information or memorizing facts someone else told me were important. Once I became mentally stimulated and tapped into my natural gifts— which had been inactive for periods of my life—I suddenly felt active and alive again. Prison has a strange way of awakening things in a man.

In prison my wits and senses became razor sharp. My mind was fertile and ready to be impregnated with knowledge. As time progressed, my mind underwent a true mutation regarding the importance of education. I came to understand that there are two types of education: the education you get in school and the one that you give yourself. Both are necessary. The education I gained through life's experiences and from reading, exploring, and thinking like a philosopher was more powerful than the one I acquired in school.

The act of studying in prison is unique in itself. Ironically, in some ways it was easier for me to study and learn in prison than it was in a traditional learning environment such as a high school or college. There are fewer distractions in prison. There are no wives or girlfriends distracting you, crying children wanting to be picked up or fed, or overbearing bosses harassing you about being late while you try to study. On the other hand, I had to develop the concentration of a monk and the discipline of a Navy Seal to study in the midst of the yelling and screaming, violence and tension, fights and riots, and the fog of hopelessness and despair that flooded the prison.

Although I certainly would have preferred studying from my home office or private reading room, prison afforded me more time to comprehend complicated concepts such as Einstein's theory of relativity, algebraic formulas, and the profound philosophical questions posed by Plato, Dr. Frances Cress Welsing, or the Egyptian Mystery System.

One of the main things I had to learn about myself was my most effective way of learning. There are supposedly seven primary styles of learning: *visual*, which uses pictures and spatial learning; *aural*, which responds to sound; *verbal*, which uses speech; *solitary*, which is self-study; *kinesthetic*, which is learning through use of hands or body parts; *logical*, which focuses on reasoning; and *social*, which is learning through group interaction. Understanding your own learning style is an important step in the learning process. I am most productive when combining all seven; however, I feel most competent when I read. Although practical, hands-on experience is very important, I was in prison and limited kinesthetically, so I had to rely on visual learning, particularly reading.

Even before I went to prison, I was moderately well-read which is atypical for a drug dealer. I had done a decent amount of reading growing up, and I did fairly well in school. I read the *San Francisco Chronicle* newspaper as well as magazines such as *Time* and *The Economist*. I had an extensive library at home with books such as *Assata* written by Assata Shakur and *Think and Grow Rich* by Napoleon Hill. I hung out in places like San Francisco's Marcus Book Store, the oldest Black bookstore in the

United States, as well as Barnes and Noble. Whenever I visited a new town, I would visit the city's top bookstores. In Portland, Oregon, I loved to visit the world-renowned Powell's Books.

Many days I would hang out for hours at a bookstore, then head out to sell someone a kilo of cocaine. On days when the snow was nearly knee-deep in Minneapolis, I would hang out at a bookstore, sipping hot chocolate while crouched in the corner with a book by Terry McMillan or John Grisham. Within minutes of leaving the bookstore, I would transform from a library-card-carrying bookworm to a gun-carrying drug dealer.

In prison I read everything I could get my hands on, from the *Wall Street Journal* to books on religion, philosophy, health, science. Through reading, I became intimately acquainted with well-known thinkers like Dr. Cornel West. I was captivated by "the double consciousness" theory of W.E.B. DuBois and fascinated with the witty wordplay of Shakespeare's sonnets.

In terms of my overall educational process in prison, I spent hundreds of hours interacting with inmates who had master's degrees and PhDs from major universities around the world, including Ivy League institutions. Many of these men were ex-college professors, NASA scientists, former high-powered international dignitaries, major CEOs, politicians, or attorneys. My interactions with them were similar to what takes place in any institution of higher learning: an exploration between teacher and student, with me playing both roles when necessary.

Engaging and discussing different educational pathways, schools of thought, and various disciplines with these men helped me understand that nobody has a monopoly on knowledge and truth. As Malcom X said, "The truth doesn't change, only our awareness of it does." There is no one line of reasoning or one perfect way to do things. We all operate through different systems and understandings.

Many of my most powerful educational moments came through

storytelling and dialogue, with the most weighty of these being an intensely interesting conversation with an old German Nazi. This guy used Hitler's autobiography, *Mein Kampf* (*My Struggle* in English), as his personal holy book. I had only seen actual Nazis in the movies and was shocked and stunned that he was still alive, but when I talked with him, the "education" I received was mind-blowing and unlike anything I could get in a traditional school.

The literature and books I read were censored and controlled by the prison. One day a correctional officer (CO) was conducting a routine search of my cell and stumbled upon *The Fountainhead* by Ayn Rand. He confiscated my book and told me I wasn't allowed to read books "like that." I asked what he meant. He replied, "This is a book for thinkers and we don't want you to learn how to think; thinkers are a threat to the security of this institution and to the United States."

From that point on, I started to hide books in the prison chapel and other places. I believe the CO's line of thinking, informed by prison policy, can be traced back to slavery when Blacks were whipped or killed for learning to read and write. In 1830, the North Carolina General Assembly passed legislation prohibiting education for slaves, and several other states had similar laws. These patterns are in keeping with James Baldwin's idea that "The victim who is able to articulate the situation of the victim has ceased to be a victim: he or she has become a threat."

In prison, my books and literature were my most prized possessions. Reading was what kept me stimulated and inspired. Books allowed me to transcend and escape my environment and soar high above the razor-wire fences. When reading, I could vicariously walk the halls of Congress and sit in the chambers as they passed the Civil Rights Act of 1964. I could walk with Jesus as he was persecuted and stoned. I could hunt wild gazelles in the savannas of Africa. Reading allowed me to psychoanalyze

Sigmund Freud and explore the minds of great thinkers who had walked the earth thousands of years before me. Although I was physically confined, reading allowed me to create a different reality for myself.

18
LET THE GAMES BEGIN

It's almost 5 a.m. I open my eyes and scan for danger. It's all good. I feel momentarily safe and secure. I am awake and alert and ready to attack the day. I start by taking ten deep breaths. With every exhale, I become a little more calm and concentrated. After about thirty minutes of focused breathing, I feel pretty peaceful, considering my circumstances.

As I finish my breathing exercises, a CO walks by. He's conducting a mandatory 5 a.m. population count; his military boots pound against the tile floor. The sound of his keys jingling and boots stomping racks my nerves. Suddenly, he stops and shines his flashlight directly into my face. I think he's trying to remind me that I am register number 09393–041 and that I am powerless.

Beneath my breath, I sarcastically mumble "thank you" to the CO; he doesn't know it, but his act of contempt strengthens me. Every small sign of disrespect that I experience in prison stokes my flame because I know that my ultimate retaliation and reprisal will come when I get out and start helping at-risk youth avoid prison.

By 5:30 a.m., my bunky is starting to toss and turn. He will be up soon, and the tension will begin. Living in an area the size of a closet with another grown man is very uncomfortable and awkward. The two of us can barely stand at the same time without bumping into each other, and we can't avoid smelling each other's breath and body odors.

To avoid a potential confrontation, I try to be gone when he gets out of the bed. Less contact equals less conflict; most inmates automatically know to give each other as much time alone in the cell as possible. As he opens his eyes, we momentarily stare at each other. The very first moment we make eye contact is critical and tense. This split second is the crucial moment that will dictate our interaction for the rest of day. I think to myself, *Is there going to be added tension today?* For a few seconds, there is stony silence, but my mind is racing.

Is he in a bad mood? Is he feeling sad because his wife recently filed for divorce? Is he stressing because his mother is dying of cancer? Is he down and depressed because he has been in prison for fifteen years and has ten more years left to serve? How will I react if he acts aggressively? And vice versa. We eye each other carefully; it is silently understood that either of us can snap without warning. He finally breaks the ice. "Today is a good day. I have a visit today. My sister is coming up from Los Angeles with my children; I haven't seen them in ten years." I indifferently tell him to enjoy his visit as I walk out.

This brief exchange lasted for only a few seconds; although fleeting, the encounter was tinged with hostility that could have led either of us to explode. Throughout the history of prisons, many prisoners have killed their bunkys and cellmates. Violence and fights between cellmates happen frequently. The interaction between cellmates is a mental game of intellectual one-upsmanship. It's a cold war; this is low-intensity warfare.

I left the cell around 6 a.m. I knew that in an hour or so the rest of the prison would be wide awake, with guys moving and maneuvering about and the hustle and bustle of prison life in high-volume swing. The youngsters would be playing their rap music, and ESPN's SportsCenter would echo through the housing units. Games at the domino and card tables would inevitably lead to frivolous arguments over who is better—Kobe or LeBron. Organized chaos would ricochet off the prison walls.

Let the games begin . . .

19
PRESSURE MANIFESTED

Dizzy and lightheaded with an unfamiliar, tingling sensation in my left hand, I realize the left side of my face is completely numb. I also have a paralyzing migraine that sends shockwaves through my left eye socket. *Am I having a stroke?*

In 2005 I found myself in prison in Florence, Colorado, after being transferred from Waseca Federal Correctional Institution in Minnesota. Florence, nestled deep in the mountains, looked like it belonged on a postcard. However, the realities prisoners lived inside the prison betrayed the picturesque scenery that surrounded the facility.

Being in prison made me sick. Literally. From the first day of my incarceration my mind and body rejected the unnatural environment. I knew it would be a difficult journey, but I was relentlessly determined to be mentally, spiritually, and physically defiant if need be. I vowed that I would not be broken.

However, as the years dragged on, I began to experience a variety of medical problems that threatened my existence in every way. The illnesses weren't life threatening or terminal, but they impacted me deeply and forced me to confront the truth about my mortality.

My conditions were not so surprising, since prison leaves very little opportunity for an individual to thrive and be healthy. Negative stimuli are everywhere—from the toxic talk and threats of violence by other inmates to the punitive energy exuded by the prison staff. Over time, an abundance of negative stimuli can and will deaden the senses.

Prison deprives its inhabitants of the sweet and stimulating scent of a woman, the uplifting sound of a child's laughter, and the vibrant color of a fresh flower. The monochromatic and monotonous realities make prison an extended sentence of sensory deprivation, which is known to harm the mind, spirit, and body.

For me, being in prison was mostly intellectual warfare, but that battle took its toll on my physical well-being. "Thought is the cause of it all," as the proverb goes. Everything starts in the mind—even our emotional and physical well-being can be influenced by a single thought. Eventually, I would find out how powerful the mind was in relation to my humanity, but prior to learning that lesson, there was a particular three-year period when I seriously doubted I would actually survive prison.

Migraine headaches became a consistent and relentless companion. On day two at Florence, I developed a horrible ear infection. My ears were constantly ringing, as if I were underwater. I felt dizzy. Initially, I thought my symptoms were just indicators of regular stress, but after a few days the pain became unbearable.

After a week, I went to prison medical. When I went to see the physician's assistant (PA), I didn't expect much. Prison PAs are known to have elementary experience and a very limited knowledge base. Prisons typically hire PAs from countries whose medical standards are much lower than those in the United States. To make matters worse, the doctors are only slightly better than the PAs and usually lack any professionalism. Many have lost their licenses or practices in the "real world," but they can exploit obscure federal laws that allow them to practice "prison medicine," using the prison population as their personal set of guinea pigs.

During my initial visit to the PA, I was humble until my medical complaint was met with indifference. My attitude didn't change anything. "Wade you are fine; take two aspirin," the PA told me. I walked back to the housing unit, agonizing over the dark reality that I could have nine more years to serve under such poor medical care.

My medical issues persisted, as did the prison medical staff's indifference to them. Over a period of approximately two months, I visited prison medical two to three times a week. The prison staff eventually threatened to lock me up in the hole if I continued to request medical attention.

As the days passed, I felt my condition progressively worsening. My lymph nodes swelled, and the glands in my neck protruded slightly and were painful. I developed sharp pain deep inside my armpit where the nodes are located. The nodes in my groin were sore and tender to the touch. I developed flu-like symptoms; my nose ran constantly, and my hacking cough was generating green mucous. I knew that problems with lymph nodes could be indicators of cancer. A little fear started to set in.

One day while walking in the prison yard, I broke out in a cold sweat. My legs shook, and I felt nervous. There was no one around to help, as the yard was closing and everyone had gone inside the building. Feeling that I couldn't take another step, I sat on a nearby bench to catch my breath. Somehow I got the strength to stumble back to the housing unit. I finally got back to my bunk and lay there sweating as my body jerked. *What the fuck is going on with me?*

When my body finally stabilized a bit, I was able to get up and take a shower, although my wobbly legs barely held me up. After the shower I staggered back to my bunk and lay there feeling drained and physically beat down. As I lay in my bunk feeling lifeless, I seriously thought about my future.

The next morning, I saw a diabetic prisoner who had been denied his daily dose of insulin lapse into a diabetic coma and drop dead directly in front of the medical building. Witnessing his death multiplied all my fears. All I could think was, *"Lord, let me make it out of this place alive."*

After seeing this unnecessary death, I began to have far more extreme and negative thoughts about my future. Although I tried to stay positive, dread and dismay continuously crept into my thinking. I imagined I was suffering from a rare form of cancer or some undiagnosed debilitating disease. My thoughts ran wild.

Nevertheless, because I was still in prison, I had to mask any visible sign of weakness or vulnerability—physical or emotional. Miraculously, I somehow maintained my commitment to routine workouts because I was convinced that I had to project a macho exterior to preserve my sense of manhood.

Although I worried about an undiagnosed major illness, I didn't need the advice of any medical expert to understand that the majority of my ailments were stress-related. The cumulative effects of being a fugitive from the FBI for seven years followed by a fourteen-year prison sentence created a millstone that began to crush me.

Gradually, I began to realize that I was not indestructible; I was human. I started to realize that I, like every other human, had a breaking point. I was a mere reed that could snap at any moment, whether in prison or out, and I was desperately afraid I had reached that moment. I felt my body was betraying me and did not believe I could continue to endure the strain, the emotional fatigue, the physical stress of pretending to be intense and unyielding every waking second.

Several months passed without any real medical attention, and I decided I would have to apply some pressure to get proper care. I filed a complaint against the prison's medical staff. I recruited people on the outside to generate more pressure, and my family, friends, and organizations that supported prisoner's rights began calling the prison repeatedly. I even wrote my state representative, California Senator Barbara Boxer, who generously replied.

I came up with another desperate strategy with the help of a friend, D-Slim, a member of the Swans Bloods gang from Los Angeles. D-Slim agreed to walk frantically to the administration building, pretending he had found me unconscious on the floor of a prison classroom. I figured the more theatrical the performance, the better chance I had of being rushed to the hospital. I had to make it to the hospital!

When the prison staff responded, I was laying on the floor pretending to be limp and lifeless. The CO seemed to sense it was a trick and shrugged indifferently. He made a half-ass attempt to help me to my feet and instructed D-Slim to escort me to the administration building.

There, the prison PA nonchalantly examined me and said, "You are okay, Wade." I weakly snapped back, "I ain't okay; I need to go to the hospital!" After about an hour, he sent me back to the housing unit with a couple of aspirin.

The next day I made several urgent phone calls to my contacts on the outside and requested that they bombard the prison warden with phone calls demanding that I be given proper medical attention. After about a week of constant pressure from my family, the prison caved, and I was finally escorted to an outside hospital.

Prison staff are reluctant to escort prisoners to the hospital for obvious reasons; an inmate could be using the hospital visit as a ploy for an escape attempt or some other kind of plot that could compromise the security of the institution. So, prison staff typically escort inmates to the hospital only in the case of grave injuries resulting from fights or riots; massive heart attacks or severe strokes; or for cancer treatments or other scheduled medical procedures. Even in these special cases, itineraries and schedules are meticulously planned to avoid an inmate making an attempted escape. The locations and times of the appointments are never shared in advance. Prisoners are whisked away abruptly and secretly.

My trip to the hospital was an interesting journey in itself. I hadn't really seen society in five years other than on a heavily guarded prison bus when I was being transferred from prison to prison. The bitter irony of the trip was that in order to move out into the free world, I was shackled from waist to toe and escorted by two armed COs.

At the hospital, we were escorted to a special elevator for prisoners. I felt like a condemned man as I duck-walked through the lobby in shackles, chains, and my prison uniform. Onlookers shot me suspicious looks and whispered in not-so-discreet tones.

When I finally made it to the doctor, a battery of tests awaited me. First, I was given an MRI of my entire central nervous system—brain, neck, and spinal column. They were seeking spots or lesions on the brain that could indicate brain cancer, signs of stroke, or ruptured vessels from hemorrhaging or a potential aneurysm. They also ran countless blood tests, checking my blood cells for markers that could signify diseases. After the tests, I was escorted back to the prison to impatiently await results.

After several weeks of sleepless nights, I hear my name over the prison announcement system: "Wade, report to medical." My heart pounds rapidly as I walk toward the medical building to get my test results. The medical building is less than a one-minute walk, yet I feel I've been walking for at least a mile.

The medical building is empty, eerily quiet, and dark. The conditions unnerve me. *Is this some kind of omen?* The nurse appears suddenly from the back office, spooking me. She asks me to sit down.

Skipping any small talk, the nurse calmly reports, "Malik, you have spinal stenosis."

"What is spinal stenosis?"

"It's a spinal condition that causes pain throughout the central nervous system. It starts from the brain and goes down the neck and into your spine and can affect your entire body."

I quickly reveal my number-one concern: "Can I die from this condition? Is it cancer-related?"

Her response relieves me, erasing death out of my mind for the moment. But there's bad news too. It's not a fatal condition, she says, but it is a painful one. But I will be getting medication to control the symptoms, she assures me.

I breathe a huge sigh of relief, but I still have many questions. So I go straight to the prison law library to do some independent research on spinal stenosis.

Prior to prison I had never taken any medication in my life. Yet at one point in prison, I was taking six different prescriptions! I was popping pills for high blood pressure and high cholesterol, antibiotics for the ear infection, a pill for gastritis (because my body rejected food), a pain reliever to control the spinal stenosis symptoms, a steroid inhaler because of a constant sinus infection, and a second steroid inhaler for asthma symptoms.

This is one of the many ways prison strips a man of his pride and humanity, leaving him symbolically naked and defenseless against the elements that assault his immune system. His body becomes porous and receptive to disease, foreign pathogens, and viruses.

Looking back, I now believe that the vast majority of my conditions were psychosomatically induced—simply the result of being in an unnatural environment that caused trauma to my mind, body, and spirit that eventually manifested into observable physical symptoms. Thought was truly the cause of it all, but to put it plainly, my thoughts were sick because I was in jail, which meant my body became sick because I was in jail.

20
RELIGION VS. SPIRITUALITY

My religious experience in prison was based on what I considered spiritual faith principles. While I certainly believe in a higher power and a force much greater than myself, I choose not to label or box myself in to a particular religious denomination, group, or school of thought just to make others feel more comfortable. At the time, I felt that being deeply rooted with a strong faith in the God of my understanding would keep me focused. I didn't take a traditional religious route.

Religion is prevalent and very popular in prison. By law, members of all officially recognized religions have the right to practice their beliefs while incarcerated. Christians and Muslims are the two dominant groups, with Jews comprising a small but powerful community as well. I chose to stay open-minded and engage in dialogue with individuals from all religious and spiritual backgrounds. I read various texts such as the Bible, the Quran, the Talmud and Torah, the Book of Mormon, and the Egyptian Book of the Dead. I also read the classic Chinese text Tao Te Ching as well as the Upanishads to get at least a partial understanding of Hinduism. I was able to extract some valuable information from all that I used to increase my overall spiritual understanding.

Prayer and meditation became a huge part of my daily spiritual practice. However, as I was praying early one morning, a CO came by my cell and shined a bright flashlight directly in my face. The light blinded me momentarily, but when my vision became clear, I could see that the CO was smirking. Suddenly, he banged his metal flashlight against my steel bunk and screamed in my ear, "WHAT ARE YOU DOING?" I was on my knees, crouched over, so he could clearly see I was either praying or meditating. It was obvious he was trying to agitate me. Although it was five in the morning and pitch dark, I could recognize his aggressive posture as he stood in front of me. We had a split-second stare-down, and then he abruptly spun and stomped away, mumbling belittling remarks.

Religion is all that some prisoners have to help them keep their sanity, and they are willing to do whatever is necessary to protect it—even kill over it. Religion helps some maintain their minds amid the thick despair and depression of prison.

There are many benefits to practicing religion and spirituality in prison. I have met guys who came to prison as gang members with thirty-year sentences, cold-blooded killers with a fire in their belly for fighting and ruthless violence, who changed radically as they became involved with religion or spiritual groups. Many of them started to significantly calm down, becoming humble and peaceful.

As in the larger world, religious backbiting between different religions exists inside prison as well. Sometimes the tension between groups is even more intense because the groups live in such close proximity and have to share one centralized chapel. Prison politics can play a large role in who gets to use the prison chapel on which days and for how long.

Religious groups tend to isolate themselves from each other in prison—as often happens outside, as well. Despite this separation, fierce spiritual debates sometimes break out. Some debates would last all day long about the *scripter* in the Bible or different Hadith or Suras in the Quran. To a degree, I understood these debates happened primarily because prisoners have unlimited time on their hands with nothing better to do. "I have nothing but time," is a frequent prisoner mantra. As a disclaimer, I believe that many prisoners do actually believe the doctrines that they promote.

At the time, I thought it was senseless to insistently evangelize and try to force someone to see things from my personal perspective—or for others to try to make me see their way. On the contrary, I wanted to learn as much as I could about different religions and spiritual pathways. However, the hostile and bitter prison environment encouraged many religious guys to spew their views with an undercurrent of aggression, dogma, and rhetoric that bordered on violence and made their views indigestible for me. I vowed not to engage in the intense religious discussions and arguments.

Ironically, throughout my prison time, I was unofficially labeled a Muslim by other inmates and the prison staff. From my understanding, the definition of Muslim is simply someone who submits to the will of God; by that definition, a person who adheres to God's laws could technically be considered Muslim. Unfortunately, however, today the term Muslim more often than not carries a negative perception by those who are ignorant of the definition in its true form.

I have had prison officials discriminate against me, profile me, call me in to the lieutenant's office for questioning, and threaten to throw me in the hole based simply on my name. My father considered himself Muslim, and my birth name, *Malik*, suggests that I am; it is an Arabic name that means *king* or *ruler*. However, I did not consider myself Muslim in the classic definition, so I found profiling by prison officials puzzling as nothing in my file indicated that I practiced Islam in prison or prior to prison. I especially came under scrutiny after the terrorist attacks on 9/11. I was called in and questioned based simply on my name.

Others like me—Black with Muslim birth names who didn't classify ourselves as Muslims—were also racially profiled. Several of these individuals were placed in solitary confinement, some indefinitely for many years. Guys with names like Hakim and Khalid were hounded and harassed based on their names, rather than their religious practices. Not so strangely, many people thought (and many still do) that I am Muslim because of how I carry myself and because I stick to a diligent prayer and daily meditation schedule several times a day. Although my father and many family members are Muslim, I choose not to limit myself.

With my current understanding of religion and spiritual practices, I prefer to focus on a person's positive principles and core beliefs that I can share rather than create divisiveness based on our different spiritual beliefs. Unfortunately, I have seen religious groups of all races in prison conduct themselves as gangs and "spiritually gangbang." On Sundays the Christians would go to church, while Muslims and others, such as Rastafarians, Jews, Asatru, and Mormons, would have their respective services on Fridays or Saturdays. On occasion I would respectfully support some in their endeavors or special events. I have spoken at some of these events, such as special ceremonies for the Rastafarians or Moorish Science Temple, and actually helped some of these groups file grievances against prison officials to get religious accommodations, such as special meals and recognition of certain religious holy days.

Ultimately, I can honestly say that my faith became much stronger once I got to prison. Mere rationality can't explain how I was able to maintain my sanity and avoid being physically hurt or mentally broken by the prison system itself.

Arriving to prison with many years to serve, it would have been easy for me to abandon God, like I saw many others do. Such was the case with a young Crip I met named Toothpick. Toothpick was distraught over his thirty-year prison sentence, and his attitude was usually doom and gloom. He denied any existence of God or a higher power and was an avowed atheist. Although I didn't agree with Toothpick, I respected his space. Ironically, the day before Toothpick and I were being transferred to separate prisons, we had a very deep discussion about religion and spirituality. Oddly, it seemed as if he was starting to slightly change his atheistic views, igniting in me—and Toothpick—a bit of hope that someday he just might believe in something greater than himself.

21
MASTER STUDENT

Yo, where you from? I'm Young Gino from Richmond, South Side, Fifteenth Street."

I intentionally ignored his statement and extended my hand sternly to introduce myself. It wasn't an accident that the young man was trying to let me know he was from Richmond, California, a city with one of the highest murder rates in the United States.

Then, unexpectedly, he ambushed me with a barrage of questions. "What prison did you just transfer from? Was a fat dude with dreadlocks named Jon Jon from Richmond there? How much time do you have? Who just got killed in Oakland?"

I sarcastically told him I had been in prison for over ten years and didn't have anything exciting to talk about. I didn't know the local neighborhood gossip, prison rumors, or any scandalous scoops. I was far removed from knowledge of anything that happened on the streets or—for the most part—in prison. Frankly, I didn't give a damn about Jon Jon or anything or anyone else that was irrelevant to my life.

For over a decade my life had consisted of carefully navigating the minefield of prison: staring eye-to-eye with hardened convicts;

praying I would neither get my head split open or split open somebody else's head in a riot or fight; and fiercely clinging to my sanity as I tried to stay alive mentally, spiritually, and physically.

When you arrive at a new prison—no matter who you are or what your reputation is—someone is going to "hit you up," which means someone is going to ask your gang or clique affiliation or what city you are from. During the initial cursory conversation, your interrogator is unofficially interviewing you as he mentally makes associations and assumptions that could potentially be used against you later. Your response could dictate the tenor of your stay at a particular prison.

Your first few minutes in a new prison are the most tense and critical. If you appear confident about yourself, you may be able to keep the predators at bay—for a while at least. If you are trembling and timid, start praying and hope that God will have mercy on you. The questioning of a new inmate can be peaceful and nonthreatening, but the inquiry can also swiftly turn deadly if the new arrival turns out to be an informant, claims the wrong gang, or encounters avowed enemies at the new prison.

Most often though, the Q&A is carried out because inmates are sensory deprived and yearning for some sort of mental or emotional stimulation, whether negative or positive. Very rarely do they ask about things such as the nature of the economy, interest rates, or the educational system. Instead, they want to know all the scandal happening on the streets: Who has recently been killed? What neighborhoods are at war? Who is the hottest rapper on the streets?

For over ten years I had refrained from this sort of conversation, totally submerging myself into intellectual and spiritual enlightenment, education, and personal development. I had very little mental space for bullshit, frivolity, or irrelevance. Although I was new to this particular prison, I knew the drill. Ironically, being in prison for ten or more years almost automatically grants you a level of respect and a certain unspoken status in the prison hierarchy. Prison society has its subtle—and not-so-subtle—shades of classism and unofficial rank system.

Based on our first conversation, I could sense that Young Gino was enthusiastic about meeting me, because my hometown was near his. In prison, particularly federal prison, where prisoners come from every state in the United States and territories such as Guam and Puerto Rico, it was comforting to meet someone from within 500 miles of your hometown.

We were at a prison in Oregon, more than 800 miles from our respective cities. But because we had grown up in the same metropolitan region, by prison rule, we were *homeboys.* Homeboyism is a major thing in prison and frames the basis for prison politics and policy, formal and informal. Although I was from San Francisco and Young Gino was from Richmond, a relatively small town about twenty minutes away, the two cities were acknowledged in prison as allies and unified as far as prison politics and the unspoken prison code of conduct were concerned. On the streets, the two cities had a similar street swagger and mentality.

After we talked for a while, Young Gino offered me a jailhouse burrito. Although prison burritos were typically bland and tasteless, they were a coveted delicacy to guys in prison, who rarely had access to good food. The taste of the burrito was irrelevant, but the gift was a sign of respect and an invitation from the homeboy. It was an unofficial welcome to the neighborhood—no different than a new neighbor in the suburbs bringing a meal to the new family on the block. I reluctantly but humbly accepted his goodwill gesture and scarfed down the burrito. I had just previously been confined in the segregated housing unit—the hole—for a while awaiting classification and had shed several pounds.

He also offered me a few personal items such as a bar of soap, lotion, toothpaste, and deodorant. As I was in transition, I would need these things until my property and personal belongings arrived from the previous prison, which could take several weeks. Normally, it was bad policy to accept anything in prison and I rarely did so. However, there was something unique about Young Gino; he had a youthful and innocent charm and seemed eager for some positive stimulation.

The next day he walked up to me as I stood in the line waiting to go in the chow hall. As we chatted, he asked me if I needed a good book to read until my property came. I told him no thanks. I was a serious reader and very particular about what books I read and whom I accepted books from. As we stood in line, he shared a bit of his background. He was twenty-one and doing five years for a drug charge, which he said saved his life by getting him off the streets. He said he wanted to change. For some strange reason I believed him. As he vented, I didn't talk much. I just looked and listened closely.

As the weeks went on, Young Gino would seek me out in the yard and come over, sort of smiling, and we would talk. He displayed a sincere interest in seeking knowledge. Observing him as he maneuvered around the prison, I could see he was different than some of the other young guys who were proud gang members. I would observe Young Gino reading or walking the prison track alone in deep thought, minding his own business. He reminded me of myself. I sometimes felt like a proud dad as I saw how he carried himself maturely, with respect for others. He wasn't loud and obnoxious like most of the gang members his age.

Gradually, we started to have more conversations, and the nature of our conversations slowly turned to serious topics such as spirituality, the meaning of life, and manhood. I was pleasantly surprised to learn Young Gino had some very interesting perspectives and that he was quite intelligent and well-read in many areas. On many occasions, I would just sit back and listen and learn. Many of his thoughts displayed a deep level of wisdom.

His thinking represented the character and opinions of a generation of young, inner-city Black boys and teenagers across America who had profound insight into the world, yet felt they hadn't been heard. I allowed him to be heard. His voice, fire, passion, and rebel spirit represented the voice of young Black, Hispanic, Asian and other youths in the inner cities of America—from South Central Los Angeles to the Bronx to the South Side of Chicago. All were inseparably linked.

Over time Young Gino began to document his thoughts, writing essays on different topics and asking me to proofread and edit them. I was impressed with how his beautiful words of poetry displayed the brainpower of a seasoned philosopher. What made Young Gino most impressive was how he continued to persevere and transform himself despite his very challenged background. He was raised by his grandmother, had a brother who was in prison for murder, and had a cousin who had been mercilessly gunned down and killed.

Over time, we would walk the prison track together, testing each other's philosophies and intellectually sparring. It wasn't always pretty, but it was beautiful because we didn't pull any punches; we kept it real. We would have ferocious debates about Malcolm X, Socrates, and the effects of hip hop music lyrics on the youth.

We both grew immeasurably during our mental jousting sessions. I can honestly say that I believe I learned more from Young Gino than he from me. I learned the real power of the youth. I learned how powerful their spirits are. I learned that the youth have the answers to many of the problems that professors and politicians haven't been able to solve for hundreds of years. As the old proverb goes, "Out of the mouths of babes comes the truth."

Over the course of two years, I saw a gradual but total transformation in Young Gino, and I started calling him the "young hood philosopher." As he started to soar above his peers in prison, he began watching less television and doing more reading. Watching his growth motivated me even more. I was nearing the end of a long bid in prison and starting to put the finishing touches on my life's masterwork. I would be out of prison soon, and I wanted to be as polished and prepared as possible.

At this point, I started writing articles and essays to be published in the newspaper when I got home, and I would go to Gino for proofreading and editing. I respected and valued his opinion because he had no problem being critical about my work. He would push me and challenge many of my long-held assumptions. He made me re-examine my value system. During this process, I learned that he had been the master teacher all along and that I was the student.

I learned age didn't take precedence over true knowledge or the passion of the youth. I can vividly remember one particular occasion when Gino gave me some sound advice after a confrontation with my bunky caused me to get uncharacteristically indignant and irate. Like a wise elder, he came and spoke with me, calmed me down and helped me put into perspective everything I had to lose.

When it was time for him to be released, I was confident that he was ready. I knew he would go on to do great things. When he left the prison, it was as if Gino were symbolically graduating Magna Cum Laude—not just from prison but from a "real" institution of higher learning. This would foretell his future.

Ultimately my prophecy came true. When Gino got out, he immediately enrolled in a community college. Within two years he graduated with his associate's degree and a 4.0 grade point average. He was subsequently accepted to UCLA on a full-ride academic scholarship, appointed to a prestigious chairmanship of a campus organization, and accepted to law school.

Young Gino has become a highly sought-after guest speaker and lecturer at colleges and universities throughout the United States and is the proud father of two handsome sons by his beautiful wife. We talk often, and he frequently expresses tremendous appreciation for me helping him change the course of his life. I feel he gives me too much credit—his gifts were inborn. They only needed to be nourished.

I may have played a minor part, though, and I am humbled and thankful that God gave me the opportunity to learn from Gino. Unknown to him at the time, he became my driving force and motivation to get released from prison and work with youth.

However, change doesn't come without challenge. I think back to a particular situation one day when Gino furiously walked to my housing unit and asked me to come outside. My heart rate accelerated; in prison you never know when a friend may need you "to put your boots on." This simply means drama is in the air and that you should be ready for a red alert, such as a fight or riot. Just moments before, Gino had been involved in a confrontation with a Bloods gang member from Los Angeles. Gino was highly upset and ready to rumble. He asked my opinion. I said one thing: "You have less than a year left. Be smart." At this point, we both expected to be out of prison soon and this was a major test to see if we both had truly changed our mind-sets and matured.

From a warrior standpoint, I respected the fact that he was willing to stand up for himself and not back down from any man. Gino weighed only 150 pounds on his best day. The other combatant was nearly 300 pounds of muscle with a dangerous demeanor and a reputation for being a bully. Ultimately, I escorted Gino over to his housing unit and helped settle the beef.

By the end of our prison journeys, Young Gino and I both had learned that the way to win almost any battle was with the mind. We chose a bigger weapon: our intellect. We chose not to use our fists. We put down our guns and picked up books. The mind, we learned, was the true weapon of mass destruction.

PART II
RETURNING, RELEARNING, RESTORING

22
A NEW WORLD

It's around 4:30 a.m. and my chest tightens with anxiety as I stare blankly at the screen of my MacBook Pro. Learning how to navigate the Internet after so many years locked away from such technology makes me feel like an alien in some far-away, futuristic world. Sometimes I feel like I have been ejected from a time machine.

Figuring out how to use today's technology is like learning a new language. Quite honestly, my first experiences with technology after leaving prison filled me with dread and anxiety. Nevertheless, I stand amazed at the ways technology has revolutionized and transformed the world during the past twelve years. Everyone seems to be engaged and preoccupied with it—overly immersed in this new thing called Facebook, and it seems everyone but me has an iPhone, iPad, or iPod.

I've only been out of prison a short while, and I'm figuring out the basics, like how to download apps. I still can't believe that you can instantly send a text message

> to someone in seconds! Even email blows my mind. In prison we used snail mail; it took days to send or receive a letter. Thinking about it makes me chuckle like a child.
>
> I have Facebook, Instagram, and Twitter accounts, but I rarely use them. The thought of exposing myself to the world overwhelms me. But the concept of Google search fascinates me. In prison it took me months, sometimes even years, to find a single piece of information. Everything I ever researched in prison came from a hardcover book, magazine, or some type of newspaper. The lightning speed of the Internet is incredible!

Learning about all the new technology presented a real challenge as I tried to adjust to life after prison. The other big challenge was relearning how to talk with "regular" people. By nature, I'm stern and serious; and in prison I was assertive and aggressive for self-preservation. After prison, however, I felt the need to be warm and welcoming when I met new people at work, at the gym, or simply standing in line at the grocery store.

I didn't know how to make small talk anymore, and I felt awkward and self-conscious when I tried. In prison, communication is usually very serious and direct and often carries an undercurrent of animosity and tension. Direct eye contact can be interpreted as an attempt to intimidate or worse.

Sometimes I felt people would be distrustful and defensive if they knew I had been recently released from prison. Although I didn't particularly think they should view me differently, I could understand their reservations and doubts about me— to an extent.

Ultimately I would have to learn to trust people and to believe that most people are genuinely good folks—not everyone is a potential enemy combatant. I was slowly learning to drop my guard and my defense mechanisms. But no matter how I acted, I always felt like I was wearing a scarlet letter—a huge and highly visible sign on my forehead that read *CONVICT*.

I spent most of my time working, readjusting to society, and planning for my future. Subconsciously, though, I was always confronting the realities of being a federal felon, of feeling like there was always an invisible hand hovering over every move I made, waiting for any excuse to snatch me back up and send me back to jail. I would get unexpected calls and unannounced visits from my probation officer. I had to wear a GPS tracking device on my ankle so they could track my every move. I was subject to a strict curfew and prohibited from traveling outside of a thirty-mile radius without contacting the federal probation office. I felt like I was going to be watched and closely scrutinized by the Feds no matter what I did for the rest of my life.

One day I left the probation office at 1 p.m. Around 1:15 my cell phone rang. It was my PO (probation officer) wanting to know where I was. She gave me instructions to go home immediately. I told her I was riding the bus and it would take me at least ten minutes; she gave me five. She was waiting by my front door when I arrived, sweating and out of breath from running from the bus stop. "Where were you? What were you doing? Who were you with?" Humility failed me, and out of frustration, I blurted out, "I just left your office fifteen minutes ago!" She told me to report back to the probation office first thing the next morning.

Spending more than a decade in prison affected my behavior and made me question my place in the world. At times I tended to try too hard to fit in and to pay too much attention to my aura and appearance. I was sometimes too attentive to my mannerisms, diction, and pronunciation—wanting to make others feel comfortable. Ironically, this is in direct contrast to the social etiquette in prison, which is dominated by body language, meta-messaging, and manipulation. Many guys in prison intentionally display bad manners and characteristics to make others think that they are crazy. In prison, ironically, crazy is good. It's a survival tactic.

But I wanted to be different than the average ex-con. I wanted to be a camouflaged butterfly that could blend into different environments, converse with different types of people, and speak articulately when need be. I wanted to be able to nimbly navigate Silicon Valley, Stanford, or an afternoon at a family picnic. Yet I also wanted to be able to easily blend back into the hood and casually kick it with youngsters on the block.

When I first got out of prison I was sentenced to a federal halfway house for ten months. Although I was technically still incarcerated, I was allowed out into society for a few hours a day to run errands, but I had to report back promptly at a prearranged time. The halfway house was similar to prison in small ways, such as mandatory count times, a roommate, lack of privacy, and horrible food.

On one of my first day passes from the halfway house, I went to look for a job. It felt strange to walk out of the building unescorted, without handcuffs, and without anybody monitoring me. I actually couldn't believe it. The halfway house was in downtown San Francisco, right in the middle of a neighborhood called the Tenderloin—the worst neighborhood in San Francisco. It was inhabited by homeless men, dope fiends, and derelicts—an unofficial outdoor insane asylum with hundreds of mentally ill people wandering around talking to themselves. It also included the biggest open-air drug market in the city.

My first day out, I strolled through downtown San Francisco for hours in amazement. I was like a child at Disneyland, mesmerized by the new rides. I felt like a naive tourist. I was so happy to have my freedom that I gave spare change to the homeless bums and talked to the mentally ill people as they talked to themselves. As I roamed the streets, I daydreamed; I window-shopped; I did it all! Wow, freedom!

I aimlessly wandered for hours, but lost track of time; I suddenly realized it was close to curfew and count time back at the halfway house. I would have to run to make it back on time. I got back to the halfway house sweating from running and physically and emotionally drained from the sights and sounds of San Francisco. As I walked back into the building, reality kicked in. I was technically still in federal custody. I was turning back into a pumpkin like the carriage in the story of Cinderella.

After the newness of being back in society started to subside, it was time to focus on getting a job. I needed money badly to eat and take care of my personal business. It took me a while, but I finally found a job in nearby Oakland. The job was at a group home for adults who were drug addicted. Taking the job was very humbling. It only paid minimum wage, and I wasn't used to taking orders from anybody in the free world; I had never worked a legitimate job in my life.

I would leave the halfway house every day by 6 a.m. to make the nearly one-hour commute to Oakland. I rode the subway for about twenty minutes, then walked for another thirty minutes through the gritty streets of Oakland. My job was in a neighborhood called Funk Town, an area that was murderous when I left for prison, but had calmed down a bit since. Nevertheless, it still carried a stench of death and danger. Daily I would walk by the liquor store and pass the young hustlers who lurked in the morning mist with pistols poking out of their North Face puff coats. Recently the area had experienced a rash of robberies, so I had to stay sharp and be on my toes. Robbers are always looking for a new victim, and I was green and freshly home—not as street sharp as I used to be.

Although it was humbling to ride the subway and walk to work, I didn't mind. I loved being able to get out in the elements and meet new people and gaze at the pretty female traffic cops directing downtown traffic. Ultimately, the travel to my job was therapeutic and calming; it helped me slowly transition back into society.

Taking that first job was a good re-entry icebreaker, but the job didn't last long. The company was having financial difficulties and ultimately couldn't make payroll. I worked there for several months but never received a check, so I had to move on.

My next job was as secretary at a community center in the Potrero Hill projects of San Francisco. Potrero Hill was like most projects in the United States: crime-ridden, decrepit, and with a desperate populace. Every day, I caught the bus to work and walked by a crowd of young gunners hanging out in front of the building where I worked. The first day I went to work, several of them were hanging outside smoking weed and listening to music. As I approached, they paused momentarily, eyeing me suspiciously, trying to sense fear or imminent threat. They sensed neither so symbolically gave me safe passage.

The job wasn't difficult, but it required that I do things I had never done before, such as filing and making folders, using the copy machine, sending faxes, and answering the telephone professionally. I was grateful to have a job, but I was getting barely above minimum wage, and I had to pay the halfway house 25 percent of my check for room and board. After expenses, I barely had enough money to eat every day, cover my transportation expenses, and pay my cell phone bill. I lasted there for a while, but after a few months a job became available that paid a whole two dollars more an hour. I jumped at the chance.

It turned out to be the most challenging job of all. It was at the nationally known, notorious Sunnydale housing projects, also called the Swamp. Sunnydale was the most violent public housing development in San Francisco. The people in Sunnydale had a different look in their eyes. Their facial expressions suggested despair and deep desperation.

I had grown up only a few blocks from Sunnydale and hung out and hustled there when I was younger, but there was a new element that had permeated the projects while I had been gone. Sunnydale's murder rate was through the roof and rising. It was treacherous terrain that felt eerily threatening and intimidating. The danger was obvious; you felt it the moment you stepped your first foot inside it.

In order to make this work, I would have to carefully use my charisma and politic my way through it. My job at Sunnydale was as the recreational specialist, which meant I would be dealing directly with the kids. The kids in Sunnydale had some of the most difficult issues in the city. Many of them were fatherless or had at least one parent on drugs, incarcerated, or murdered. Although I was all too familiar with this pattern, this job would still be a challenge for me. I had to pause and ask myself, *"How will I react if physically challenged? How will I respond if blatantly disrespected?"*

Kids in Sunnydale—and kids in San Francisco in general—were unique in terms of their inner-city pedigree. In San Francisco there was no strict street code of conduct or clearly defined hierarchy in the hood. The street politics were unlike any other major big city in America. There were no Crips and Bloods or Gangster Disciples and Vice Lords, all of which have an unmistakable presence in every major city in America. There was no "Big Homey" or "OG" to listen to or call the shots or make decisions for the guys in the street. There was no organized system to which younger guys deferred. Therefore, young folks had an independent, self-governing mind-set and temperament that symbolically said, "I don't give a damn who you are, or how much time you served in prison, or what your reputation was; this is *my* neighborhood. Shut up, come to work, and don't tell me shit." I respected it. I wanted to live.

Fortunately, I still knew many of the older guys in the neighborhood who were able to peacefully persuade the young guys to grant me safe passage. Although I wasn't physically scared of the kids and didn't let them completely run amok in the center or disrespect me, I dealt with them wisely and warily.

Working at Sunnydale was not easy. Sometimes I would have to close down the center and leave after 9 p.m. The lights in Sunnydale had been shot out, so it was dark and spooky. I didn't have a car at the time so I relied on the bus. As I waited for the bus, my senses would be on high alert. I would suspiciously scan every car that drove by as my central nervous system stayed in fight or flight mode—like being in prison during times of tension and high alert.

In the back of my mind I was always careful about the potential of a youngster wanting to "knock down" or kill an OG who had done a lot of time in federal prison. Although it didn't carry the same weight or the same amount of respect as knocking down a rival from another neighborhood, you would still get military stripes in the street and shoot up in the ranks. The irony in it all was that I was a nonthreat—as peaceful as a dove and only concerned with making enough money to survive and returning home safely.

Fortunately, I had a family member who was the executive director of the recreation center and the unofficial mayor in the area, which indirectly indicated that I was safe. Working in Sunnydale was humbling because, upon my initial entry into this unique ecosystem, I had to walk on eggshells. I had come into an environment that already had its street politics and protocol and the stimuli that it was used to; anything or anybody that came and interrupted the order of things could be subject to elimination. Unfamiliar stimuli or unwelcome ideas could be met with deadly disdain; thus I had to remain humble.

I learned another important lesson during my experience in Sunnydale; I discovered that the streets are for young men, not forty-year-olds. I knew my place and stayed in it. Although I did do some good work and provided some mentorship and guidance for a few youngsters who were willing to listen, I didn't force the issue or pry into anyone's personal business unless we had a relationship and rapport. When negative conversations took place and war stories were debated and discussed, I didn't rudely interject. If I did intervene, I did so peacefully and diplomatically. I learned how to stay in my lane.

Eventually I got a car and was able to drive back and forth to work. My first car after release was given to me by my friend Terry Rollins. The car was a 1993 Chevy Camaro; the interior was raggedy and ripped to shreds in several places; it had a big dent in the driver's door; the doors didn't lock; and worst of all, it didn't have a reverse gear. It was a far cry from the 400 SEL Mercedes Benz that I was driving at the time of my arrest. Nevertheless, I was grateful that I didn't have to walk or catch the bus anymore.

Overall, the entire experience of re-entering society was a blessing and a great learning experience. Sometimes as I reminisce and try to put the entire experience in perspective, I simply laugh to myself and say, "Damn, things sure have changed."

The days of being a big-time baller are gone now. I am no longer "The Guy"; someone else is. Today I am a Regular Joe; I know because I now have to pay close attention to price tags when grocery shopping. I wince at the price of a carton of milk or a dozen eggs or when I am unable to repair my car because of insufficient funds in the bank. Today I keep money in my wallet. I don't keep cash in huge trash bags like I used to. I now have days when I have to impatiently wait on payday to simply pay bills. I've learned that penny pinching is an acquired taste—one that I don't like.

When I first entered prison, my hair was jet black, healthy, and wavy. Today I am as bald as a bowling ball. Women don't blush or bat their eyes at me the way they used to. Today I am older, grayer, and a step slower; my swagger is outdated by some standards. I just sit back, smile, and laugh at myself. Because I am alive and free, and that is the most important thing.

23
STAYING FOCUSED

As I walk down the street, I peep over my shoulder. I have a weird, but familiar, feeling that I'm being shadowed. Out of my peripheral vision, I see someone approach me.

"How did you know that I was out?" I ask, surprised.

"I know everything."

We stare at each other momentarily, size each other up from head to toe, and then hesitantly hug as we both burst into laughter.

I used to connect with Amigo when I was selling drugs. I hadn't seen him in twenty years. While I've been away, Amigo has still been out here on the streets. Somehow he managed to avoid a life sentence in federal prison. Although I'm not sure what he's into these days, I have heard stories. I reluctantly decide to give him a few minutes of my time. I am leery about being seen with him, but I think—or rather hope—that maybe he has turned over a new leaf. He's an old friend, and it's actually good to see that he is alive and free. Mentally, however, I put my guard up, instinctively scanning the streets, surveying my immediate environment as a safety precaution. Just in case he is being followed by anybody.

"Come on, my car is parked across the street."

"No thank you, Brother; let's walk." I know better than to be fresh out of jail and get into a car with someone with an infamous reputation for being a dope dealer. Technically, I am taking a risk by simply walking and talking with him.

We casually walk around downtown San Francisco for a little while, catching up on old times before he abruptly asks if we can find a restaurant to sit down and eat. He says he wants to talk to me about something important. My heart starts to thump a little bit. Amigo is a shrewd businessman who is always looking to make some money. I know he has an ulterior motive and some sort of angle. I just hope that it is something legal and legitimate.

This is my first big test, and questions race through my mind. *Is he going to proposition me to get back into the life? How I am going to react if he asks me to work with him? Will I respectfully decline? Will I resist temptation?*

Selling drugs is no different than any other addiction. The triggers, signs, and symptoms of addiction for me are emotional and behavioral. But my biggest trigger is old acquaintances still in the life, so staying away from them is my goal. It is mentally unhealthy and harmful for me to hang around or interact with friends who wear $50,000 watches and drive $100,000 cars. Nobody is immune to being triggered. Therefore, I consciously choose to avoid certain environments where criminal activity takes place. *I must stay focused.*

I kicked my addiction of selling drugs cold turkey while I was in prison, but I was able to do so in large part because in prison I was not exposed to my triggers: the temptation of making millions of dollars, the seduction of beautiful women, and the allure of vast amounts of material possessions. Although it seems that I was forced to quit selling drugs, there was actually a lot of wheeling and drug dealing in prison. It was just like the outside world except the quantities were smaller and accessibility was not as easy.

I had stayed away from selling drugs in prison. But could I stay away from selling drugs in society? That would be the ultimate test for me. Selling drugs was all I knew.

Amigo and I slyly size each other up while we walk, trying not to make each other feel uncomfortable. We silently scrutinize each other, secretly probing for pressure points that might draw a verbal or nonverbal reaction or other cue. It is a cunning and covert mind game. As we talk, it's obvious that he is doing well. He looks healthy, well groomed, and content, but I also know that part of this is a front. Drug dealers are masters at bluffing. I know the level of the game he plays comes with continuous trauma and tension. And, undoubtedly, heat from the Feds.

The common denominator between Amigo and me is that we have respect for each other under the umbrella of "honor among thieves." He appreciates that I am not an informant and that I steadfastly refused to cooperate with the government when I was arrested.

He knows I took full responsibility for my own actions and did not incriminate or point the finger at him or anyone else.

I have chosen not to be bitter that neither he nor any of my former criminal associates wrote or sent me money while I was in prison. I understood that criminals are extremely reluctant to stay in contact with guys in prison for fear of attracting unnecessary heat. Actually, it was better for me not to associate with them either, for a couple of reasons. This ensured I was not indirectly implicated in any of their dealing that could have made me guilty by association. Some of my friends wound up with a new conspiracy charge and received an additional twenty years. Cutting off contact with Amigo and the others had also made it easier for me to stay mentally focused and heal. Being in jail offered the opportunity for a clean break.

Amigo and I eventually stop to eat at a nice Italian restaurant. We talk informally about his new businesses, his homes, and his travels around the world. In his distinct Spanish accent, he says, "Wow, you sure have changed. You were always quiet but you seem even more so."

"Yes, I am a lot more focused and thoughtful now. I had a lot of time to think."

Based on our conversation, I speculate he is still in the life. Suddenly, mid-sentence, Amigo abruptly drops his utensils, stops chewing his food, looks me directly in the eye and asks, "Are you done?"

I know exactly what he means. This is the question I was hoping he wouldn't ask me. He is consciously trying to trigger me and push my emotional buttons. He is asking if I am done dealing drugs for good. I stare back at him. As we lock gazes, my chest begins to tighten and I suddenly feel dehydrated. Things seem to slow down around me. Although the stare-down is brief, it seems as if we look into each other's eyes for minutes. Fortunately for me, Amigo does not intimidate me, as we both have a powerful presence and strong will, and our relationship has always been based on mutual respect.

But slowly, rage starts to boil beneath the surface of my stone-cold facial expression. I am offended—though not necessarily surprised—that he would ask me such a profound question after not seeing me for over twenty years. *Who the fuck does he think he is, asking me to risk going back to prison for the rest of my life? He hasn't served a day in prison!*

I have been home only a few short weeks from a twelve-year blow in a federal facility. Technically, I am still in federal custody, living in a group halfway house. If I make even a minor mistake, I could be sent back to prison immediately. No questions asked.

I finally respond verbally: "NO! I ain't interested in your offer." I rise to leave, but he gently grips my forearm and asks me to hear him out. I tell him that I have to be back to the halfway house soon and that if he knows of anybody with a legitimate job offer, to have them call me. He pleads for me to at least sit and finish my lunch. I reluctantly sit down and quickly change the subject; we continue to talk casually.

As I finish my food and rise again, Amigo jumps up, paces along beside me, and begins to proposition me one last time. I feel like a prostitute with a persuasive pimp. He says he is willing to start me on consignment with twenty-five units of cocaine at $20,000 per unit. This means I would owe him $500,000, to be paid back as soon I make the money back. I am mad as hell about his proposition for a couple of reasons. It's a selfish sign of disrespect on his part; why did he think I would work for him in the first place? I had always worked for myself. I stare at him blankly as he says his final piece, then coldly walk away. I tell him to be careful and send my regards to his family.

As I walked back to the halfway house, I was disillusioned and disturbed. I felt insulted and angry at Amigo for propositioning me although I knew guys like him were self-centered and cared about only one thing: M-O-N-E-Y. I was also proud that I had been secure in my self-esteem and had not allowed myself to succumb to his scheme. *Had he planned and plotted on me for all of those years?*

Prior to prison, I had been somewhat ignorant to the legal and social penalties of dealing drugs. I didn't completely understand the serious nature until I was actually in federal custody. After serving such a long prison term and intensely studying drug laws and the inner workings of the prison system itself, I thoroughly recognized the entire picture. I ultimately realized I had been just a puny pawn on the world's chessboard, being used by an invisible force much bigger than myself. I also knew I would never knowingly be used as a pawn again; I'd never be left in the lurch as the million-dollar fall guy. Somebody else would have to do the Devil's work.

Even though I had made a lot of money during my drug career, who actually benefited from it? Certainly not me. My entire criminal career had been a nerve-racking nightmare that led me to the FBI's fugitive list and a fourteen-year federal prison sentence. Countless lives were destroyed in my wake; my actions contributed to the devastation of my community and nearly fatally shattered my familial relationships. My drug career definitely didn't end happily ever after. Most of them don't.

When I got back to the halfway house, I checked in, went straight to my room, and collapsed limply on the bed as my thoughts raced uncontrollably. I knew I had made the right decision, but I also knew I would have to pray and deeply meditate to continue to stay strong when I was fully out in society. I knew that I had to be resistant once the daily struggles of everyday life started. I would have to take it one day at a time, just like all recovering addicts do. Amigo would not be the only person who could be a potential trigger. I had to be careful and cautious of my environment and associations.

Being on federal probation was somewhat of a defense mechanism for me because I was strictly prohibited from being in contact with anyone who had a criminal record. This was the greatest irony of all, as most of the people I had grown up with had gone to prison or been on probation or parole at some point in their lives. This was also true of many of the people in my immediate family. I had to be very strategic about how I navigated my associations and friendships.

Although I had learned in prison how to live a humble existence, surviving on just the basic necessities, it was still a huge mental adjustment to be nearly penniless in society. It's easy for people to say, "Just be happy to be free and out of prison." But living in society is not free.

Safeway and Pacific Gas and Electric are not free. Groceries need to be purchased, and bus fare and gas are not handed out with thirty-day invoices to be paid later, unless you have credit, which I did not have after being locked up. In prison, you have free room and board, and you don't have to pay for cable, AT&T, or an iPhone. Being home and starting completely from scratch, struggling to survive, was one of the biggest mental adjustments I've had to make.

However, if I did not learn to adjust, I knew I would fall prey to the seduction of the next Amigo who crossed my path—which would be a ticket back to prison for the rest of my life.

24
PRISON'S IMPACT ON RELATIONSHIPS AND SELF

Mass incarceration produces devastating effects on the entire community on many different levels, and the far-reaching ramifications affect us all. Of course, as an individual, I am most deeply affected by the damage done to my familial relationships over the course of my journey.

When I went to prison, my daughter slept in a crib. When I returned, she was a freshman in high school. Today's awkward and clipped conversations with my daughter and her one-syllable replies to my questions demonstrate the disconnect between us. Too much time has been lost—time that I can't get back.

How do I alleviate some of her anger and resentment about my long absence from her life? How do I open my heart to her and share my emotions so that she will feel validated and loved as a young lady? Daughters need that love from their "Daddy" so they can operate in the world with high levels of self-esteem. Unfortunately for me, there is no do-over. I will never be able to push her in a swing at the park, read her a Mickey Mouse bedtime story, or attend her ballet recitals.

How do I let her know how intensely guilty I feel about the pain that I caused her by being derelict in my duty as a father? Attempts to pour out my heart have proven unsuccessful. She doesn't realize that I hurt, too, and that her rejection is painful to me and her reluctance to open up hurts me deep down inside. She is my only child. She has 50 percent of my DNA and half of my chromosomes. And from what I hear, my daughter has some of my mannerisms and the same serious look on her face. In the end, however, the burden and responsibility is mine to make things right, since I am the one who made the decisions that led me to prison and that ultimately caused this situation in the first place.

The woman who waited and endured the entire twenty-year struggle with me has understandably been upset and deeply affected by my time in prison. Bitterness has festered and hardened her heart, even though she was the one who made the critical decision to wait on me for all those years. Although she deeply cares about me, sometimes her resentment manifests itself in terse tones and emotional eruptions.

But before I blow up at her, I try to pause and put things into proper perspective. I try to understand and humble myself. How many women would actually wait for so many years—especially for a man who was not her husband? I can't blame her for being upset; she has lost and sacrificed a lot. She put it all on the line. She gambled and placed a bet on her future. It was a calculated risk. In the twenty years she spent waiting for me, she could have gotten married to a handsome husband and raised beautiful children. But she chose to wait. She waited on the unknown because it was a mystery to all of us about how I would feel and act when I returned.

When we have troubles, I have to ask myself, "Would things be the same between us if I hadn't left? Would it still be such a struggle?" No woman should have to endure such emotional torture. I take personal responsibility for much of her torment, for I was selfish and manipulative. If the roles had been reversed, would I have waited? Probably not. I owe her much respect for staying in my corner.

One of the most disturbing and overlooked consequences of incarceration is the prevention of procreation while a person is in prison. For many years, I was not able to produce a child, possibly preventing the birth of a child who would eventually become a doctor to find the cure for a disease, or a leader of the people, or a politician who would write new laws and legislation that could benefit society. Every day while I was in prison, millions of my sperm died. The dreams and visions of my potential children will never be realized. I will never know if those sperm would be the next Muhammad Ali or Maya Angelou.

The lasting effects of the break-up of the family through mass incarceration are devastating—no matter the color or community that is affected. However, according to a White House report titled "Economic Perspectives on Incarceration and the Criminal Justice System, April 2016," Black families suffer from this experience at higher rates than others.

From the beginning of our existence in this country, the Black family has always been on fragile footing—prone to being scattered and separated and held in bondage. In the 1600s, when slaves were viciously kidnapped and brought to the U.S., families were immediately split up and sold at the slave auction block. For example, the father may have been sold to a plantation owner in Georgia, the mother to a slave owner in Louisiana, and the children to different plantations in Florida and South Carolina. This pattern was repeated throughout the centuries of slavery in our country; when slavery was outlawed, economic factors often forced the separation of Black families.

No other group in this country has that legacy. With the exception of the indigenous natives of this land, others came here as willing immigrants. Although groups of people have come here fleeing political and religious persecution, their choices were nevertheless voluntary. Unfortunately, the breaking up of the Black family has been part of the legacy of this country. Now mass incarceration is part of that legacy as well.

Like many others who have gone to prison, I am traumatized. The dictionary definition of trauma is "an experience that produces psychological injury or pain." Though I may not visibly appear traumatized at a glance, based on my own self-diagnosis, I experience post-traumatic stress disorder (PTSD) on two different levels. First, I am afflicted with an injury that happened previously but which continues to cause me pain today. And second, I suffer from "prison traumatic stress disorder," a disorder directly linked to prison. There is a subtle nuance between the two.

Due to pride, many men are hesitant to say they experience PTSD. Others simply may not recognize it. Although I am highly functional in all areas, there are moments when the subtle side effects of PTSD show up in the form of becoming immediately defensive and preparing myself for a fight or other type of confrontation when it is not necessary.

Now that I am back in society, I would be negligent if I didn't express my deepest concerns about the potential long-term effects of my prolonged absence. I attempt to ignore the supposed scarlet letter of a felon, but subconsciously it may bother me more than I like to admit.

Sometimes I feel like a stranger in a strange land here. Due to my personal growth and development while I was in prison, family, friends, and past acquaintances don't understand many of my new and evolved viewpoints. My long absence and shift in thinking make it nearly impossible to talk to old friends, many of whom have been beaten down by life, divorced, shot, stabbed, or robbed of a bit of their sanity through the daily struggles. I genuinely inquire about the health and welfare of their family members when I see them, but when we part ways, I know that something has happened along the way to both of us. Things will never be the same.

Today, I have to deal with the reality of not having a lot of money anymore. This is constantly a mental battle for me. When I was first released, I was reduced to the salary of a pizza delivery boy making minimum wage with no tips. Before prison, I had acted as a president of a very lucrative corporation. Had I not been strong-minded in the initial stages of my release, I would have been back in the saddle selling drugs nationwide at full throttle again—with my old drug connect Amigo at my right hand.

However, for many reasons, I can't sell drugs again. My spirit won't allow it. With my greater understanding of the context of the big picture, I know now that I was a naive pawn. The game was over before it began. The winner was already decided.

Since my release, I wake up to attack the day with a vision to change my community. I know that some young man somewhere needs my guidance and can learn from my many mistakes. I have over forty years of good examples of bad decisions to share with him.

Part of my drive, fire, and passion comes as a direct result of one moment in the hole in the federal penitentiary at Terre Haute, Indiana, as I awaited transfer to another prison. After nine straight days of lockdown without a shower, toothbrush, toothpaste, toilet paper, or soap, I smelled so bad that I couldn't stand myself. I felt filthy, like a caveman; it was the lowest of the low. Roaches crawled around the cell. The COs left the light on all night, making it even harder to sleep. The plumbing was so old that the water wouldn't turn off completely, and the hissing sound drove me nuts.

To make matters worse, I was in the cell with a big grizzly of a man with a life sentence and a horrible attitude. He and I were ready to literally kill each other. The stress of the situation was crushing, and I was a powder keg ready to blow at any minute. This scene gives me my stubborn mind-set when I am faced with adversity today.

Remembering those days motivates me and inspires my motto: *My plan has to work!* Terre Haute penitentiary is not an option.

According to a spiritual proverb, "Man is truth and falsehood strangely mixed." I take that to mean that man is a riddle; he can't be completely figured out. I was hardened in prison but I was simultaneously softened. I was hardened over the years by the often harsh, petty, and punitive treatment, but I was also softened through cherishing childhood memories and by learning about the deep need to empathize and develop a level of understanding with self.

25
BERKELEY

My name is #09393–041. The reason I introduce myself as a number is because I just recently finished serving twelve years of a fourteen-year sentence in federal prison. As far as the United States government is concerned, I am not a human being; I am just a number.

That was how I opened a presentation at University of California at Berkeley. Being invited to lecture and co-facilitate a class at such a prestigious institution was a humbling experience. Although I had prepared for the occasion for many years, the reality was nerve-racking.

The chance to speak at UC Berkeley came about as a result of a correspondence I developed with a Berkeley professor while I was in prison. The professor reached out to me through a special program backed by the university's African American studies department. Along with several other inmates, I had submitted essays and writings to Berkeley for a special exhibit that was meant to highlight the undiscovered talents of those who were incarcerated. My essay, "Incarcerated Intellectual," was chosen from many entrants to be featured and discussed.

Although the professor was a talented, smart, and beautiful woman, the correspondence between us was purely platonic. She provided me with much-needed scholarly stimulation in a world otherwise devoid of such. In turn, I provided her with an alternative set of perspectives and insights to help prevent her from becoming academically nearsighted. Over the years, we nourished and fed each other philosophical food—food that served to satisfy my enormous appetite for knowledge for many years throughout incarceration.

As I rode the BART subway train across the bay from San Francisco to Berkeley, I intensely studied my speech notes. Even though the lecture was based on my personal story, there were particular bullet points that I wanted to address. And I wanted to be perfect in my delivery without sounding too scripted and artificial. Studying during rush hour was no easy feat as the train jerked and jutted forward, starting and stopping abruptly. The guy sitting next to me reeked of urine and garlic. People tiredly trudging home from work created an atmosphere of stress and tension.

Once I got off the subway, I walked through downtown Berkeley toward campus. After the jerky subway ride, my stomach felt a bit uncomfortable so I stopped and got a slice of pizza from world-famous Blondie's Pizza. As I continued, I let the sights and scenes of Berkeley fill my senses.

Berkeley is beautiful and deservedly famous for its distinctive Bohemian carefree spirit and uniquely diverse environment. This wasn't my first time in Berkeley, but it was the first time that I actually paid close attention to its eclectic character. Dreadlocked children on skateboards zigzagged aggressively through traffic; old hippies, who looked like they could still be protesting the

Vietnam War, passed out flyers promoting socialism; students casually strolled down the streets, openly smoking marijuana while simultaneously carrying loads of books; bald Buddhist monks demonstrated peacefully side by side with Jewish priests. The scene seemed unreal.

As I got closer to campus, I ran into a huge student-led march and rally. I had to shove and elbow my way through the demonstration as they shrieked and shouted for the firing of UC Berkeley's president. This was a completely different universe . . .

When I finally got to campus, I inhaled, admiring its natural beauty. I walked around, looking for a nice quiet place to sit and collect my thoughts. I found sanctuary under a redwood tree that easily rose over 200 feet. I sat on the ground, crossed my legs, closed my eyes, and meditated. The environment felt calm and tranquil. Although there was lots of movement around me, I was oblivious, relaxed, and completely comfortable. I was sitting on a patch of brown dirt only partially mixed with grass. The dirt slightly stained my pants, but I didn't care. I was at peace. I felt as if I could have slept there the remainder of the night.

My mind naturally reflected on how this current environment contrasted with previous environments: the constant chaos of prison; the years running from the FBI; dangerous drug deals in city streets all over the country. But at that particular moment, I felt free and liberated.

I opened my eyes and closely watched the students roaming about. I smiled to myself in admiration as I envied their nonchalance and naiveté. Their movements were smooth, fluid, and carefree, reminiscent of Chinese elders who practiced Tai Chi. My daydreaming over, I just sat back and soaked it all in. I took ten deep breaths; on the last breath I deeply inhaled the environment through my pores and all five senses. I wanted to absorb every bit of positive energy the campus had to give.

I put on my Beats by Dre headphones; I wanted to hear some music to further enhance my already blissful state of consciousness. I played one of my favorite songs: Jill Scott's "Brotha." As I repeatedly listened to the song, I increasingly became strengthened and inspired. The lyrics describe the struggles of being a Black man in the world and promote perseverance through adversity. I felt the lyrics epitomized my life.

The students in the classroom are staring at me with rapt attention. Their eyes penetrate me. They sit motionless, hanging on every word I speak. Their body language subliminally invites me to captivate them and continue feeding their curiosity.

More students gradually filter in, locking eyes with me as soon as they enter. I sense that many of them have never before met a man who had been to prison. Their intrigue is written all over their faces.

The energy in the classroom is electric, yet the professor does a great job of moving the conversation forward and making me feel welcome. A camera crew is filming me; although they are friendly and unobtrusive, I can sense that the camera guy is somewhat distracted and absorbed in my story as well.

As I speak, I feel genuinely acknowledged and accepted by the students and staff. There is no sense of an exotic curiosity syndrome; I do not feel over-scrutinized or judged. I feel safe to share my ideas. Several professors from other departments sit in on my lecture, taking the opportunity to listen in and respectfully provide context and additional framework to the discussion.

The lecture itself is a mutual process—a give and take. By listening and exchanging ideas, the students move me more than they can imagine. I become their student in the same way I became Young Gino's student in prison. Through their nonverbal cues, they educate me. I learn from their penetrating and profound questions, and I learn about the power of being inquisitive. The entire exchange is poignant and powerful—a moving human moment that can only be experienced firsthand. This is not theory. It can't be read in a book. This is education in its essence.

My lecture is titled "Black and Male in America," and it shares its name with a class that Professor Quame specifically designed around part of my life's journey. The curriculum for the class includes a compilation of many of my experiences as a criminal, FBI fugitive, prisoner, ex-convict, and now a scholar. Other required readings and writings support the curriculum and lesson plan.

This is my very first speech at a major university, and I am confident but a bit nervous. *Man, this is UC Berkeley, one of the top universities in the world!* The students here are smart and informed. If I don't express myself clearly, this could become a meaningless disaster.

UC Berkeley doesn't invite commonplace pedestrians to speak. They only invite you if they think you have something profound to say. Over the years, many great speakers and lecturers have spoken here—people such as Mario Savio of the Free Speech Movement in the '60s and Malcolm X with his fiery oratory.

When I was first asked to speak, I had not been

particularly interested in the history and tradition of UC Berkeley or in its past speakers and lecturers. Although I recognized that both were quite impressive and contained lots of prestige and status, I was most enthused about the idea of positively impacting the hearts and the minds of young, bright-futured students who would be leading the world someday.

Surely, the rich and storied tradition of Berkeley has been well chronicled. To many, UC Berkeley is sacred ground—one of the most historically celebrated universities in the world. It was the command post of protest and social change in the United States in the 1960s. Sproul Plaza has been ground zero for many fights for social justice over the years.

I had prepared for this speech for many years. As I sat in prison, I had a vision that one day I would speak at UC Berkeley. Over the years as I wrote the speech, I visualized myself standing in front of crowds of intrigued and interested students. This vivid dream motivated me to practice and perfect my speaking and writing skills even as I struggled to suppress my eagerness of getting out and delivering my speech. For many years, it had remained a dream deferred.

Yet today, I am actually delivering the speech I first wrote over ten years ago! The power of dreaming!

During my speech I talk to the students about my journey on the road to redemption. However, I don't solely focus on myself. I also shift the emphasis to them. I talk to them about their associations and their choices of friends. I tell them about the many doctors and lawyers and rich and powerful businessmen that I had met in federal prison. They were serving time for making bad choices like taking bribes, money laundering, financial embezzlement, massive Medicare fraud, and—in some cases—murder.

I tell the students that they will be the engineers, politicians, and professors who will be responsible for leading the world in the coming years. But I also emphasize to them that with bad choices and decisions, they, too, could instead become the future homeless hobos, convicted felons, drug addicts, or unemployed. Nobody is immune to failure, I say.

When I finish, several students and some of the professors approach me. They want my contact information and want to stay in touch. The professors invite me to come speak in their departments, and the students ask for mentorship and guidance. I am humbled.

In the three years since my initial lecture at UC Berkeley, I have spoken there on several occasions. I remain in contact with a few students, some of whom I mentor now. While in prison, I manifested the beginning of this reality. By speaking my dream out loud, it ultimately became true.

26
MENTORSHIP

"Can you give me $100,000?"

"No. But I can make a donation of $25,000 as soon as we have the lawyer finalize the paperwork. Then, I can try to help you raise the other $75,000 that you need later."

I am meeting with one of my mentors, "Uncle Pete." We casually munch on hamburgers and fries while checking out the San Francisco Giants baseball game. He has just agreed to give me $25,000 to start my mentoring program for at-risk youth. I call it Scholastic Interest Group.

Pete and I went back to my high school days at Jefferson High School in Daly City when he was an assistant coach of our state championship basketball team. We had reconnected after I was released from prison. While I was away, Pete had become a successful businessman, but you couldn't tell by looking at him. He was an average-looking white dude, about five nine, a little thick around the midsection, quiet and low-key. He didn't look or act like someone who had money.

When we reconnected, Pete and I had several conversations about my future and what I wanted to do with my life. Although I am sure he was concerned, he didn't press the issue about my past. As far as I could see, he demonstrated no major misgivings or doubts about working with me and supporting a recently released ex-con who had been imprisoned on drugs and weapons charges.

Pete put his entire personal and professional reputation on the line to associate with me. Most well-to-do folks wouldn't take the chance. I understood that from the beginning. However, as our relationship grew and we developed a certain level of trust and mutual respect for each other, Pete started to introduce me to other prominent people and friends including attorneys, plastic surgeons, and other successful entrepreneurs. They seemed to all accept me at face value and never made me feel judged in any way. When Pete made introductions, he didn't mention my colorful background, but he gave me the option to talk about my past if I chose to.

The relationships I eventually developed with these individuals were not patronizing or phony; the connections felt genuine. Honestly, I was somewhat shocked to receive support and to be assisted by successful and affluent folks with no strings attached, since I came from the hood and my background was criminal and very much inner-city. Eventually, some of these individuals started to make contributions to my nonprofit organization.

I was certainly not a puppet being controlled or manipulated by a group of puppeteers, a situation that can develop in the nonprofit world when financial backing comes with lots of strings. Recipients of that help are expected to dance to someone else's music and to modify personal and political desires and opinions in exchange for support. I was firm, adamant, and uncompromising about my priority:

helping young African American inner-city boys without the politics and extra BS. I continue to stand firm on that.

Although laid-back and low-key, Pete and I are both very strong-willed, and we have had our share of differences. Pete is very opinionated, as am I. He is a shrewd Italian cat born in Brooklyn, New York, and far from a pushover. I've always had my own bossy tendencies as well. We have vigorously challenged many of each other's views, but ultimately we respect each other's opinions even when we agree to disagree.

One thing that I like about Pete is his willingness to admit his lack of knowledge in certain areas. Although he understands many things about life and how the world works, he is well aware that he is not knowledgeable about the inner city or some of the major issues I face every day as a Black man and a permanently branded felon.

Pete and I have an unlikely partnership. I come from low-income housing and a single-parent household. He comes from a solid two-parent household—his parents were married nearly sixty years. His friends are businessmen, doctors, and lawyers. My past friends had been dope dealers, crooks, and convicts.

Most guys from my background have never made a friend like Pete—somebody from the other side of tracks. But Pete and I understand that we make each other better in many ways. He gives me a different perspective and has introduced me to people who are not only financially beneficial to my work, but also socially stimulating in my life. I am an unapologetic and proud Black man who loves my culture, but I also like to learn about other cultures and appreciate being exposed to different groups of people. I enhance Pete's life by providing a different perspective on many levels. Our relationship is truly mutually beneficial.

Pete and I connect on a basic human level. Ultimately, it is not about your group or culture: your character and the person you are inside determine whether you will be a good friend or an enjoyable companion. In the streets we say, "Real recognize Real," whether it comes in the form of another Black man, or someone from the Samoan culture, or a hip and shrewd Italian dude, which is how I refer to Pete.

We both understand that if my parents had been doctors or lawyers who raised me in the wealthy and comfortable suburbs of San Francisco, my life might have been different. We both believe that all of us are primarily the products of our life experiences and environments and of the circumstances surrounding our upbringing.

When I got out of prison, I made a conscious choice to cultivate a second set of friends. However, I did not and could not overlook or disregard all of my past acquaintances, such as cherished childhood friends who are on the straight and living right. There will always be genuine love and concern for them as I vigorously cling to childhood memories and moments in my life I wish I could relive. Today I am deeply embedded in my community; I live in the hood, and my office is in the heart of the housing projects. But I often attend fundraisers at McMansions in wealthy neighborhoods and conduct meetings with high-powered business consultants in Silicon Valley. Both perspectives keep me humble.

I understand that old friends play a major role in my humility and remind me where I come from. However, I had to distance myself from many of my old associates with whom I had been in dangerous and life threatening situations—situations that could've resulted in my brains blown out or a life sentence. I had to leave those friends behind and love them from a distance because some of them still live that way today.

Among my new friends and mentors is Russell. Russell is a very successful venture capitalist in Silicon Valley who lends millions of dollars to people to start their businesses. I met Russell when I was in a special program called Project ReMADE at Stanford Law School. He and I hit it off immediately. It didn't matter that he was an older white dude with money. He respected me. I have been to his huge private estate and to his business and have met his family. They are good folks who are nonjudgmental. To this day, I have never asked Russell for any money. His friendship and sound business advice are worth more than money. Russell is very quiet and low-key, unconcerned with flaunting his business success and money. That is what I like about him.

Another mentor is Dr. Mark Robinson. Dr. Mark is a college professor and founder of the Institute for Personal Player Development. Dr. Mark is a genius. His intellect makes me feel like an infant staring up at an adult, but he has been very helpful, always providing me with good knowledge and wisdom. I am proud to have him as a friend and mentor, and the fact that he is Black makes me even more proud to be associated with him, knowing that he is among the relatively small group of Black male college professors in this country.

Michael Santos is yet another friend and mentor whom I greatly respect. Michael and I met in prison while he was serving a forty-five-year prison sentence on drug charges. When I first met him, I said to myself, "Dude is sharp." We immediately "recognized" each other and slyly sized each other up like two top lions in a pride. I served time with him at two separate prisons, and in both places he was one of the hardest working and most diligent guys in there. He woke up at 3 a.m. every day and started reading, working out, and studying. While in prison, he authored several books, all of which have sold very well. He was also teaching classes in the prison, and I sat directly front and center every chance that I had. Watching Michael taught me the value of work ethic. Today he is out of prison and has become one of the country's top prison consultants and most sought-after speakers on prison-related issues. I closely follow his blueprint and take many of the same steps that he has taken.

Ed Donaldson is one of my main mentors. Ed is a much more polished and sharper version of me, just a bit older. People sometimes think we are fraternal twins. Ed, too, was born and raised in the inner city of San Francisco and has overcome some major obstacles in his life. Ed is what I call an intellectual killer; he is a thinker and a shrewd negotiator and dealmaker. He is just as sharp—and often sharper—as many politicians, investment bankers, or Fortune 500 CEOs. Ed has taught me the importance of humility and deliberate thinking.

Aside from Ed, my most notable mentor is Mike McCoy, the most brilliant man I have ever met, although I have not seen him for years. I met Mike after I had been in prison for ten years; he was—and still is—serving a twenty-five-year sentence for a financial crime. Mike was a tall, Black, aristocratic dude, about six-three, 200 pounds, with a humble but firm spirit. Guys from the streets would consider Mike a square. For a Black man, he didn't have the typical inner-city background or rough-around-the-edges attitude.

Mike told me that his lack of street cred posed a problem when he first entered prison because many Blacks shied away from him. Many of the hardcore gangbangers treated him coldly because they thought he wasn't Black enough. *Bullshit.* Mike's knowledge of self and culture and vast reading exceeded that of anybody that I have ever met. He was more "real" than most gangbangers and so-called killers I've met. He just demonstrated it differently. But Mike wasn't a soft dude. He was in great physical shape, could jump rope like Floyd Mayweather, and knew martial arts. Don't judge a book by the cover!

I too might have treated Mike with disdain if I had met him early in my prison term. But by the time I'd been in prison for ten years, I was more open-minded and mature, ready to engage individuals from different backgrounds and perspectives.

Mike's knowledge was like an encyclopedia. He was a human Google search bar before I knew what Google was. It seemed as if he knew everything. Prior to prison Mike had been a very successful businessman, with a company worth an estimated $20 million at the time of his arrest. A true Renaissance man, Mike was a lawyer who also had a master's in business administration, who spoke several languages, and was a master chef.

I am forever grateful for the life lessons he instilled in me, and I appreciate his patience as he helped guide me. I am in awe at how he handled his twenty-five-year sentence with grace and humility and a big beautiful smile on his face every day.

Sometimes I would shyly walk over to Mike, like a little boy vying for his father's attention, and ask for a bit of his time. I would be timid, not out of fear, but out of respect for him and his time. Although we were in prison, he was very busy writing books, studying, and diligently preparing for his eventual release. I wanted to ask him questions about life and about how he managed to become a successful businessman.

Although usually busy, he would always stop what he was doing and patiently talk with me. He had a very subtle way of "mentally moving me," challenging me to look at things from different vantage points. I would sit in admiration as he humbly exhibited his intellect. When he talked, I always had a pen and paper with me to feverishly jot down everything he said. I didn't want to miss anything. I would often think, "Damn, they locked you up because you know too much; you are dangerous." Mike gave me the ultimate mentor experience.

It's been years since I have seen Mike as he is still in prison today. But his effect on me was so profound that every day when I wake up I spend at least a few minutes studying the notes that I took from our conversations. His life lessons will stay with me forever.

The common denominator of all of my mentors is that they are humble in their success. And they all see something special in me that they feel can be developed. When I was fifteen years old carrying a 22-caliber pistol and selling dope in a crack house in the Sunnydale projects, who would have ever imagined that I would one day have some legitimate white millionaire friends?

Things sure have changed.

Even so, I still have many friends in my own neighborhood. Everyone should have that balance of perspectives. Either extreme can be dangerous. As I was preparing to leave prison, I remember a conversation I had while walking the prison exercise track with a good friend named Art. Art was a character, an eccentric older Jewish dude whom I considered a close friend and teacher.

Art was unique. He had fathered a child with Wyomia Tyus, a Black woman who won three gold medals in the 1964 and 1968 Olympics. He was also a close friend and confidant to John Carlos and Tommie Smith, the two Black Olympic track athletes recognized all over the world for their raised black-gloved fist photo in the 1968 Olympics in Mexico City. As Art and I would talk, he would impress upon me the importance of trusting the power in my story.

One day as we were walking the prison track, I asked, "Art, what do you think is going to happen when I get out and get around those college professors, lawyers, and rich white folks?" I was not seeking validation or acceptance from anyone; however, I knew that to effectively spread my message about the plight of the inner city to people outside of my community, I would have to get out of my comfort zone.

He stared at me for a few seconds. Lowering his glasses to the bridge of his nose, he said, "Your perspective is unique. Don't forget it," and abruptly walked away. I walked away puzzled and unsure, but his words later proved to be on point. Today, whenever I feel unsure, Art's words pop up in my head and strengthen me. *My perspective is unique.*

When I got out of prison, I took Art's advice and stepped out of my comfort zone. Growth only happens when you are uncomfortable. Today, I can navigate the corporate boardroom with a suit and tie just as well as I can navigate the projects of West Oakland in a hoodie. When I walk into a meeting and talk with people who have power and influence, I feel indestructible. My life's experiences have prepared me for these high-powered conversations and negotiations. I'm not intimidated by talking with someone such as Fred Blackwell, the CEO of the San Francisco Foundation, an organization that controls over a billion dollars in assets. Perhaps surprisingly, when in these meetings, I rely on many of the skills I learned when I was in the streets: shrewd, strategic thinking; long-range vision; and gut feelings and intuition. I realize that these are all transferable skills.

That's not to say that I've never been uncomfortable in a particular environment. One day I went to a big fundraiser at a huge mansion on a million-dollar estate. When I walked in, some of the guests gave me looks that said, *Who the hell invited you?* The music was very different; the food was foreign to my palate; and the conversations were private. However, I didn't tuck my tail and leave; I stayed—not because I wanted to be accepted or liked but because I knew I could grow through my discomfort. I eventually had a nice time and met some interesting, open-minded people who arrived later. Being around people from different backgrounds is definitely an acquired taste.

I am grateful that I have been blessed with the understanding of the importance of humility and the ability to reach out to others for help and guidance. I am blessed to have a diversity of mentors and friends who bring different perspectives.

Fortunately, I have always been a leader, and I don't believe in letting anyone influence my choice of friends. In prison, the more time that I spent with certain individuals, the more other inmates whispered about my associations with "those dudes." "Those dudes" were white-collar criminals, despised by some in the prison as being arrogant and unapproachable. I felt the same way in the beginning of my prison bid, but opening up to "those dudes" changed that attitude.

Once I got wind of the whispering campaign about my friendships,

I had to confront it head-on. In prison you can't let even the smallest thing linger as it could fester into resentment, which could potentially develop into a physical confrontation. I immediately had a conversation with a particular individual and firmly but quietly told him to mind his own business and focus on serving his own time. This guy had been in thirty years; I understood he was displacing and projecting his own feelings of "woe is me." Fortunately for both of us, the discussion ended peacefully.

It would be completely foolish and small-minded of me to deprive myself of being mentored or taught information by bright business minds because the guys teaching me don't look like me or because they come from a different background or because they are Chinese or East Asian, etc. These men can possibly change my own life and the lives of my family members. The bottom line, as they say in the streets, is that "They had game." Those wealthy and successful white-collar business dudes typically had information that was much more valuable to me than what I could learn at the domino and card table from a small-time dope dealer (although some of them are sharp and worldly, too). Letting someone else choose your friends or decide your fate is foolish. If I had listened to others, I wouldn't be friends with these successful entrepreneurs who enhance me intellectually, stimulate me spiritually, and provide me with a new set of opportunities to grow as a person. I would be in the hood every day hanging out with people who talk about the same old stuff in the streets that usually leads to prison or death. Do the math.

Often, because of their own limitations and insecurities, and/or their inability or unwillingness to venture outside of their comfort zones, people will project onto you their own feelings of inadequacy that prevent them from broadening their horizons in this world of infinite opportunities.

Because of my newly formed relationships and mentorships,

I believe that man cannot figure out things alone in this world; he needs guidance—not only from a higher power, but also from those around him. Only a fool believes he can do it alone.

> A fool knows of all things but his own ignorance.
> —*Pharaoh Akhenaten*

27
STREETS TO STANFORD

I am standing on what many consider sacred ground: the campus of Stanford University. To some, Stanford represents the pinnacle of formal education. It symbolizes intellect, creativity, and genius. Famous people like golfer Tiger Woods, Nike founder Phil Knight, and former Secretary of State Condoleezza Rice have walked these halls; it is one of the finest educational institutions in the world.

The campus is stunning. The redwood trees seem as tall as skyscrapers; the landscaping is perfectly manicured. I am struck by the beauty of the breathtaking environment and by how peaceful and serene it feels. It is a completely different world than my more familiar environments of prison and inner-city streets.

As I casually cross the campus on my way to class, I notice the students nonchalantly riding their bikes, playing volleyball in the sand, throwing Frisbees, or simply joking and horseplaying in the grass. The students display a completely carefree and cheerful attitude, and

I notice their charming innocence and naiveté. But I also recognize that the students seem to subtly acknowledge a certain level of respect for each other.

On the surface, the students appear lighthearted and happy-go-lucky; however, I see serious levels of determination beneath the lighthearted nonchalance, a definite focus in their eyes. Though the signs are subtle, I can tell these students are fixated on success and achievement.

It's my first day of class. I am participating in a special entrepreneurship program at Stanford Law School called Project ReMADE. The exclusive program accepts only six to eight formerly incarcerated people per year. The intense twelve-week course promises to teach me things such as marketing, accounting, and how to write a business plan.

I am assigned a team of mentors from Stanford Business and Law Schools as well as a venture capitalist from Silicon Valley on this first day. My mentoring team and I immediately hit it off and begin developing a good relationship with a strong sense of collaboration.

A guest speaker comes in to address our first class. He's a venture capitalist from Silicon Valley who has owned several successful technology companies. His inspirational presentation helps broaden my perspectives and prompts me to start thinking on another level. After listening to him speak, I feel the possibilities are unlimited.

I have always thrived in stimulating and challenging environments, and being at Stanford is bringing out some of my best qualities—making me want to strive for excellence.

When I got to Stanford I was a bit surprised to notice that, despite obvious differences, I had a lot in common with the other students. We were all driven, focused, and disciplined. Many Stanford students had been valedictorians—top of their classes throughout their school careers. I, too, had been a leader and head of my class—as a criminal and drug dealer.

When the students interacted with me, they displayed no judgment of me. When engaging them in conversation, I felt like one of their peers. They accepted me at face value and treated me as if I belonged among them.

Over time I was able to develop solid relationships with a couple of them. When I felt it was appropriate, I shared my background with them. Surprisingly, it was always a nonissue and irrelevant. Actually, it strengthened our relationships and added a level of intrigue for them.

Even after I completed the program at Stanford, I continued these relationships, corresponding regularly with these students. I would go down to Stanford and have lunch with them and sit in on their classes and provide objective feedback on projects and assignments. This experience revealed to me that I may have things in common with many different types of people in the world, even though on the surface it might seem like we would be complete opposites and have come from two completely different worlds. At some point, I now believe, we all connect on a human level.

Every now and then before class, I would take a deep breath and reflect on the irony of being a student on the Stanford campus. In years past, I had walked around the University of Pittsburgh or the University of Minnesota with a backpack full of cocaine. I used the campuses for transactions because they were busy, making it easy to blend in. At Stanford, I carried notepads and a MacBook Pro in my backpack, walking around like any other student in my college hoodie and Nike sandals. I shopped and bought books at the campus bookstore, got a bite to eat in the café, and casually chatted with other idealistic students about conquering new challenges, investigating new start-ups in Silicon Valley, and making a difference in the world.

I would always smile inwardly and chuckle when students on campus would ask me questions like, "For what law firm are you going to go to work? Will you be starting a new tech start-up company in Silicon Valley once you graduate?" If they only knew . . .

The last day of class I had to do a final presentation. As I walked on stage and stood behind the podium, I started to get the shakes. I was speaking in front of Stanford students as well as venture capitalists from Silicon Valley who were potentially interested in investing in me or my idea. I felt as if the world was watching—like I was singing "The Star Spangled Banner" at the Super Bowl on national television. This was my big moment. If I gave a good presentation, I might get an investor to help me start my nonprofit—my dream could come true. I had to perform!

This was yet another moment I had prepared for while in prison. I knew that one day I would be speaking at Stanford, and I had written a speech for this very occasion many years earlier. When I finished my PowerPoint presentation, I got a standing ovation from the audience. My endorphins kicked in; it was an exciting feeling.

My ultimate goal and objective for participating in the program was to network and meet like-minded individuals who had access to resources that I could possibly tap into later. And I did gain contacts such as lawyers, tech entrepreneurs, Stanford professors, and business investors. All in all, the experience was something I will never forget. Now, on my résumé, I can say that I am a graduate from the Stanford Law School Project ReMADE, class of 2013!

As I look back on my trials and tribulations over the past twenty years of my surreal existence, it's ironic but true to say that my life in the streets and in prison prepared me for Stanford. Over the years, throughout my criminal career, there were many transferrable skills learned that could not only be applied to Stanford, but to corporate America as well. I am certainly not advocating that anyone endure such a painful and damaging existence to prepare themselves to succeed in life; however, my experiences in the streets and in prison ultimately were not in vain.

Often as I reminisce on the preparation of my life's final project—my self-development—I look back on the many thousands of consecutive days I sat in prison and diligently studied for ten to twelve hours per day. Many days my work went deep into the wee hours of the night, with only a few breaks for a few minutes here and there. Except for count times, breaks to use the bathroom, or meals, I would sit crouched in one position for hours on end in deep concentration. Imagine going to law school or medical school for over a decade straight without any spring breaks, summer vacations, holidays, or time off!

Looking further back, I can see that I began developing the discipline that served me well in prison when I was running from the Feds. Those years forced me to cultivate a certain amount of patience and persistence to sit still and think. The introspective thinking I did while I was a fugitive, the logical reasoning skills I developed, and the critical thinking abilities I refined had a tremendous positive impact on me. I can honestly say these skills must have been lying dormant inside me. However, it took a life-altering chain of events to activate these natural abilities—which would eventually serve me well when I needed them most. What initially seemed like a curse was ultimately a blessing.

Growing up on the streets of San Francisco, I was always a keen observer of human nature, and I always wondered what motivated individuals, particularly people in the inner city and impoverished communities. However, I also wondered what motivated people to want to be smart. What inspired people to want to excel academically or want to become successful in business and in life? I believe that the development of such motivation goes back to the controversial argument of nature versus nurture.

If I had been born as the wealthy offspring of socially prominent parents who were lawyers or doctors, would that have guaranteed that I would be successful? If so, how does that explain the case of Lyle and Eric Menendez? The Menendez brothers were born and raised in Beverly Hills to wealthy parents, who they gruesomely murdered in cold blood in 1989. On the flip side, how does someone like Oprah Winfrey, born to a maid and a coal miner in rural Mississippi, become more successful than most graduates from Stanford, Harvard, or other elite educational institutions throughout the world? Our individual paths and journeys are all unique.

Although my experience at Stanford was fulfilling and enlightening, on occasion I have seen certain individuals in corporate America and academia display arrogance because they have gone to prestigious schools. Some of them seem to suggest that their backgrounds, pedigrees, or individual life experiences are superior to mine. Certain individuals seem to believe that their attendance at an Ivy League university or Wharton School of Business or MIT makes their educational experience superior to mine.

I don't always challenge such people. I let them continue to live in their own heads. However, I feel that my experience—although it may be considered unusual—is just as rich as theirs. Actually, I believe it takes just as much, if not more, discipline and perseverance to be a scholar from the streets than to be a scholar born to wealth and privilege who benefits from a million-dollar trust fund or educational endowment.

Throughout both my street studies and my prison education, I was never preoccupied with credentials and qualifications. I wanted to be *learned*, but I wasn't concerned with being *lettered*. I was not seeking recognition or endorsement from the system or its accredited institutions. I wanted knowledge that I could learn organically and naturally.

While incarcerated, I would often suspiciously analyze the thoughts and opinions of so-called experts—professors of philosophy, sociology, and so on. This was particularly true if their opinions were based on pure theory but zero experience about subject matters that directly affected my life, such as the criminal justice system or the inner city.

On several occasions I have engaged in very vigorous discussions and exchanges with men and women who are highly regarded in the upper echelons of the academic and intellectual space. During our exchanges I have had to enlighten them about the advantages and disadvantages that I had or didn't have as I worked on my own dissertation. I didn't have the luxury of studying and researching in a traditional learning environment, such as a beautiful college campus with vast resources, an academic incubator, or a well-funded think tank. However, I can also choose to see this as an advantage, since I was less inclined to be indoctrinated, taught by way of rote memorization, or programmed by professors, so-called instructors, or the incomplete assumptions of someone else.

Being self-taught, I was more likely to objectively dissect data and information through an open-minded lens and develop lines of reasoning outside the logic suggested by professors and pundits—logic that is often put forth without conscious rebuttal by students who fear retaliation, a failing grade, critical peer review, or denial into prestigious postgraduate programs.

Studying in prison was very challenging, to say the least. Although the constant chaos and commotion of prison can be overwhelming, it can also stimulate higher levels of concentration and focus. However, there are distinct disadvantages to studying challenging and complex subject matter without feedback from experts in the field. Ultimately, I believe it's a stalemate. My journey and matriculation through the streets and prison doesn't trump the experience of anyone—nor is my experience inferior. They are simply different paths.

There are many kids in the inner city and people in prison today who have hidden genius inside of them. Unfortunately, many of them have been given few opportunities to showcase their gifts and talents. Poor parents don't have the money to send their kids to expensive camps that teach them how to write code or program computers at an early age. Sometimes something as simple as learning how to play an instrument is cost-prohibitive for poor families.

Although entrepreneurship comes naturally to many in the inner city—particularly those who become drug dealers—many of them have never gotten the formal training required to take it to the next level and become legitimate businessmen. I am a prime example of this. Although I am of slightly above average intelligence and have a solid skill set, I am conscious that there are glaring gaps in my knowledge base as it relates to business concepts typically learned in a formal academic setting from seasoned professionals. Had I been exposed to better educational opportunities when I was younger, my life might have taken a different path.

I was in awe at some of the genius on display in prison. I have witnessed hardcore killers and gang members teach themselves how to play multiple instruments. I have witnessed gang members play the piano in a way that would make Beethoven blush. I have seen inmates learn to play solos on the guitar that would make Santana smile with envy. I have observed killers with little formal education teach themselves to fluently speak multiple languages such as German, Swahili, French, and Mandarin. I met guys who have taught themselves how to write computer code and develop their own apps from the uncomfortable confines of a prison classroom.

Some people would consider my journey from the streets to Stanford as an untraditional path. In my opinion, the streets and prison served as my incubator. My science lab was a prison cell. My quad and common area were an open dorm, filled with hundreds of rowdy prison inmates. And my professors were convicted felons. Although I have never claimed to be a full-time or official student at Stanford, I nevertheless felt like I belonged for the twelve weeks I was there. I feel there are a number of others who come from similar backgrounds as myself who also belong at Stanford. The gang member belongs; he just may not know it yet.

I often ask myself what would have to change so that guys like me who come from the inner city, challenged backgrounds, and/or prison could attend universities like Stanford, UC Berkeley, Morehouse, or Howard University on a regular basis in a traditional trajectory? And how can that be considered the norm and not the exception?

The bar must be raised; there must be a shift in thinking sooner or later. When I walk through the projects daily and look at the young guys hanging on the corner, I don't see thugs or killers; I see potential engineers, architects, and lawyers. Over time I have been fortunate to develop a trained eye, and at cursory glance I can see the potential gifts in a "thug." I can see the natural charisma, the quick-witted intelligence, and the swift analytical skills, all of which translate and transfer very well into any business, industry, or school.

Unfortunately, for many of them, they will go to jail instead of Yale; instead of going to Howard University, they will become hardened convicts; and like me, instead of attending Princeton, they will go to prison. My educational pathway may be untraditional, but I view the world as my classroom and the entire earth as an institution of higher learning. I truly believe in education without borders. Figuratively, I got my associate of arts and bachelor of science degrees on the streets. In terms of defined educational pedigree, I have a PhD in being a Black male in American society with a specific focus on incarceration and the inner city. *Pressure* is my formal dissertation. This memoir is my contribution to the body of knowledge on these topics.

As a society, we must learn to be on the lookout for our young savants who are dressed in baggy, oversized clothing, sagging pants, and sporting a rough exterior. We must positively channel a young man's misdiagnosed ADHD, his misinterpreted defiance, and his misunderstood acting out. We must patiently peel away the layers to see that he has the skills to develop apps, or be a doctor or architect.

I went from the streets to Stanford. Now the tide has turned, and I am going from Stanford back to the streets, in order to help young people discover themselves and their true talents.

28
THE JOURNEY

When the FBI indicted me on conspiracy charges, my entire life was put on pause. I stepped into a time machine. It was two straight decades of suspended animation as my life slowly slipped away like sand in an hourglass.

In April of 1993, I began my life as a fugitive from the FBI. For the next 2,555 days, I couldn't dream or plan for my future. I couldn't get a legal driver's license or bank account, or establish anything for myself because I knew that I was always one step away from spending the rest of my life in prison. Closure for that portion of my life came on October 26, 2000, when I was sentenced to 5,140 days in federal prison.

Today, I am out in the free world, and I've started a new journey, a fresh beginning that allows me to roam about freely and interact with the world in a way that is natural and limitless. Today, I can breathe.

However, I have a lot of unanswered questions as I travel this new part of my path. When I first left prison, I had a lot of questions. *How will I fit into this new life of being a law-abiding citizen? How will I navigate the banking and credit system? How will it feel to have a driver's license in my real name? How will my mind, body, and soul adapt to this new environment? Where will I be in five years?*

I feel like I am twenty years behind the rest of society. I am late. Most people my age are homeowners with credit cards; most are married or in stable relationships and are raising or have raised children. Not me. The thought of starting from scratch makes my stomach uneasy.

As the days and weeks slowly went by after my release, the initial shock of being thrown back into society decreased, and I started to adjust. Catching the bus and riding public transportation played a key role in helping me get my feet back on the ground as it helped me develop a feel for city life and the neighborhood vibe.

My first ride on the subway was awkward. It took me several minutes just to figure out how to insert my money into the machine to get a ticket. As I stood there confused, an old homeless man walked up and offered his help. Initially I was skeptical; in prison if someone offers you anything, they usually have an ulterior motive. However, I humbly accepted his help. I will never forget the dirty looks of the clearly annoyed people standing in line behind me. I knew they were thinking, *You idiot! Hurry up!*

Riding the bus was an unexpectedly wild adventure. Young thugs on the bus were smoking weed, playing loud music, cussing violently, and threatening to rob the other passengers. *Please, youngsters, don't try me and make me defend myself.* I was six-two, 202 pounds, and in tip-top physical condition like a professional prize fighter, but I knew some young guys carry guns like they do their ID. I couldn't win. I decided, *I better be cool and stay in my place.* Then I got on another bus.

On bus trips, I was pressured to buy everything from marijuana to prescription pills like Xanax and oxycodone. I witnessed shoving matches and fights, yelling and screaming. Other passengers elbowed their way through a crowd without ever saying "excuse me." People would step on your brand-new shoes and then dare you to say something. There was a commotion of sounds I hadn't heard in years. It was completely nerve-racking.

I made a conscious decision to frequently ride a subway line called the T-train to get a real dose of San Francisco. The T-train went from one end of the city to other, picking up passengers who primarily worked in the financial center and in corporate America in addition to lots of homeless people who lived in and around the poverty-stricken areas of the city. The T-train traveled to the main ghetto of San Francisco, the Bayview Hunters Point neighborhood, where I was born and one of the places where I started selling dope and where I returned after being released from prison. The Bayview is primarily a poor Black, Hispanic, and Asian neighborhood.

Some days I would get off the bus or T-train and walk through the city. I would look up and stare at all the cranes and new buildings that had sprung up since I left. There were entire new neighborhoods in San Francisco, like Mission Bay and SOMA, that had not existed twenty years earlier. I stared in amazement. *Damn, you have been gone a long time.*

My very first post-prison grocery store trip nearly caused sensory overload. When I walked into the Safeway on 16th and Potrero in San Francisco, I was stunned by the whiff of fresh doughnuts from the bakery, the bright orange and blue of the Captain Crunch cereal boxes, and the mountains of fresh produce and fluorescent green watermelons. People were freely moving about and selecting whatever food they wanted. I had not been able to choose my favorite type of bread or milk for years, and having so many choices now almost paralyzed me.

As I stood in the aisle, mesmerized by the unlimited amount of choices, my fiancée called my name impatiently and tapped me on the shoulder. She told me I had looked confused and bewildered for several minutes—almost as if I were in a trance. Clearly, she didn't understand how my years in prison affected me in ways that couldn't be explained to anyone who has not experienced it.

As I navigate my new journey, every now and then, I stop and ask myself, *How in the hell did you get through that twenty-year nightmare?* Impulsively, I say *God.* I believe there had to be a higher force much greater than myself that brought me safely through. Because while I was actually in the middle of that journey, it felt like a nearly impossible feat that tested me in every possible way; and in some instances, I thought it would kill me.

How did I do it? *Blood, sweat, and tears.* The blood that was shed in prison, the sweat of nervousness, the silent and invisible tears I shed alone in the middle of the night as I thought about my grandmother and loved ones. These things will never leave me. They are all ingredients of the journey, part of the life experiences that comprise Malik, the man.

Reflecting on those years, a rush of thoughts overwhelms me as I reflect on my personal evolution, mental transformation, maturation, metamorphosis—all the internal things that people didn't see. The doubts about my existence, the questions about my purpose on earth, the shift in my thinking. I catch glimpses of the path, the journey, and the lessons learned along the way. I recall the discipline that was developed, the mental sparring with myself, the spiritual warfare, the transformation.

My bouts of wavering while in prison eventually led to a mode of positive consciousness, at which point I started to become more aware of my personal principles and standards—how they affected not only me, but others in society as well. I started to be more mindful of how I was perceived by others. I started to take into account the sensitivities of others in society.

Through it all, subconsciously, I knew that my life had a bigger purpose. I never questioned God or wondered, *Why me?* On a much deeper level, I knew that eventually I would be delivered. I knew that my purpose in life was not to be remembered only as a convicted drug dealer. So when I didn't want to read another chapter, write another line, or do another push-up, I pushed on and persevered; when I was mentally and emotionally tired, I kept fighting. I didn't want to die inside literally or figuratively; I didn't want to die spiritually or emotionally. I swore that I would not be only a shell of a man when I left prison. I would leave prison in full bloom and whole.

Spiritually speaking, my journey was necessary. I believe God gives us the will to choose and make decisions. I chose my path.

I compare my journey to alchemy, the process of transforming base or corrupted metals into fine gold. The fiery process completely engulfs you; if you can withstand the heat, your impurities will be removed. The latter is what happened to me.

Although I am far from perfect and still evolving and learning, today my moral compass stays still. My value system is intact and built on integrity, humility, and the desire to do the right thing. It is centered on the Golden Rule: "Treat others how I want to be treated." For decades of my life I repressed this moral code and chose to conspire against myself, defiantly acting out against my own best interests.

I cannot pinpoint exactly when the light came on, but after seriously reflecting on my journey, a major mental shift allowed me to start viewing things differently. I started seeing the good, the bad, and the ugly—part of the mental transformation that happened as I began reading an extensive and varied collection of books from various authors. Many of the books were both spiritual and philosophical. The books stimulated deep thought and helped me begin to objectively view the world from a different, more-informed perspective—a perspective that wasn't obstructed by the streets or obscured by the bright lights of the world.

Today I am no longer morally bankrupt, and I no longer prey on the weaknesses of others. I show compassion for the community instead of exploiting it. I try to put others before myself. I do not want to be respected as a drug dealer, ex-con, or someone with an infamous or legendary criminal reputation. I don't want to be arrogant and abrasive as I used to be; I want to be viewed as the epitome of selflessness. I want to forever shed the skin of greed and arrogance.

I embrace the journey. I look forward to life's challenges, to elevating to new planes of spirituality, and to conquering new financial challenges, such as *legitimately* becoming a millionaire. Most importantly, I plan to make a contribution that can help at-risk youth enhance their lives.

Every day now—just as I did for the twenty years I was on the run and in prison—I wake up early in the morning to strategically plan my next move. Nothing is done without careful thought and consideration. This is the third quarter of my life. As in the game of chess, I can't waste any moves, so I constantly operate with a sense of urgency. I only have a certain amount of time to get my work done here on earth.

In order to survive, I have to use all of my God-given tools: the conviction of Martin Luther King Jr., the tactics of Sun Tzu's *Art of War*, and—I pray for just a fraction of—the intelligence of Barack Obama. I must call into existence all of my natural gifts, as well as those of my ancestors. First thing in the morning, I must speak to the likes of Steve Biko, Harriet Tubman, Imhotep, Carter G. Woodson, Frederick Douglass, and others to guide me on this journey. And most importantly, I must ask for God's favor and mercy.

During my darker prison days, I would suddenly think about the years I had to serve. And a big, fluorescent number 14 would pop into my head, as bright as the sun. I would immediately go to my bunk, and lay in the fetal position as if I were a baby who wanted to crawl back into his mother's womb. I think about those days now and then.

Other times I laugh as I reflect on my journey while sitting in a nice restaurant, eating one of my favorite meals of fettuccine alfredo with shrimp and filet mignon steak cooked tender—just how I like it—with sautéed vegetables. As I sip my Shirley Temple, I smile, exhale deeply, and say, *You made it!*

Sometimes, I'll be walking the beach at dusk, just acting silly, and I will smile and let out a loud scream: *You made it!* I clap my hands as if I am cheering for the home team: *me.*

I am determined to make the rest of my life the best of my life. I would be lying if I said I'm never nervous or afraid. Fear of the unknown can be paralyzing.

How did I do it? Other than God, in the end, *humility* is what saved me. Being humble enough to sit still and listen to "the spirit." How will I continue this journey? The same way: walking humbly with God and "the spirit."

29
THE RIDDLES OF THE WORLD

"Somebody pointed a pistol at me yesterday on the bus! I don't feel safe. Can you give me a ride tomorrow?"

"No problem," I tell my young friend.

I hang up the phone and sit in deep thought for a split second about what I have just committed to. Should I have asked for more details? I have developed a good relationship over the past few years with this young man, who I had met and mentored in Juvenile Hall. I am one of the few people he can always turn to in time of desperate need.

Riding public transportation is daring and dangerous for him because he has several sworn enemies. Recently he has been implicated in a murder. Although he beat the charges, the dead man's friends and family still blame him; rumors are they have an unquenchable thirst for my young friend's blood. They are not his only enemies that make the streets unsafe for him; the police view him as a dangerous gun-toting gang member. My young friend seems prime for a spot on the evening news as the victim of a deadly shooting.

When I pick him up, I am on high alert. It isn't out of the question to think an ambush could be waiting for him. If I get caught in the crossfire, I could become collateral damage. Nevertheless, I have agreed to help him, and I plan to keep my word. However, I'm not completely crazy; I consider different scenarios for a strategic retreat—just in case things get sketchy.

I carefully circle the block before I swiftly swoop in and pick him up. I conduct counter-surveillance as I pull up, scoping the area for anything strange. I know I'm taking on a huge responsibility. He is literally trusting me with his life, counting on me to keep his whereabouts a secret while assuring his safe passage. Betrayal has never been part of my DNA, and I know how to keep my mouth shut. This scenario may seem strange and complex for a person who goes to work downtown in a regular office, but this is how I lived most of my adult life prior to prison: defying death.

The accusations being whispered in the streets about my friend are not really my concern. I am no longer in the streets; I do humanitarian work. I was no different than a doctor tending to someone who has been shot, a defense attorney defending an accused murderer, or a priest listening to the confession of a heinous or horrible act. I don't ask questions. I have to be objective and compassionate and suppress any judgments. I let the laws of cause and effect take their natural course as far as he—and others like him—are concerned. In my line of work, being judgmental could be deadly because it totally undermines credibility and hinders the ability to heal others. Young men like this one are deeply hurting, screaming out for help, and need someone to not just hear them, but to *listen* to them.

As he gets into my car, I think and act quickly. Is someone lurking in the shadows? My mind's eye becomes focused with a panoramic view of the neighborhood like Google Maps. If I am seen with him, will others in the community get upset with me for helping an accused murderer—someone with a double-crossing reputation who is perceived as a violent threat to the community? What would the dead man's family and friends have to say about me? Would the community question my trustworthiness, allegiances, and alliances?

I cautiously pull off as I brace myself to expect the unexpected. We make it safely to our destination, but I don't just drop him off. I escort him to his appointment to show him further support and stay until the appointment is over.

During our time together, I proceed with caution, dealing with him firmly, but respectfully. I am still the grown man in this situation. This particular young man is a contradiction—very talented and engaging on many different levels, but with a very dark and sinister side that appears occasionally. He could easily switch from humble to hot-blooded. He is careful, however, not to reveal this side to me and is always respectful in my presence. I am very aware, though, that he could at any minute turn venomous and strike like a snake.

As we drive back toward his home after the appointment, I don't say much, but I patiently listen to his concerns. He voices them vigorously, threatening to become volatile. Before I drop him off, I nonjudgmentally offer a jewel of wisdom: remain humble and be patient with life, I tell him. I drive away, scanning the area carefully for would-be enemies. As I leave the neighborhood, I breathe a sigh of relief that God has again covered me.

Would I do it again? No question. I have no doubts or regrets.

Although I had experienced many death-defying moments when I had been in the streets, they were situations that I could somewhat manage and control. I was generally familiar with the potential variables that could go wrong. Helping this young man pulled me out of my comfort zone because I was less familiar with the details of his situation. However, I knew days like this would come with the territory when I decided to work with youth, particularly those most at risk. I knew that I wasn't going to be working with Boy Scouts or kids who sang in the church choir. I work with young accused killers, armed robbers, and carjackers—young men who carry guns as if they are a form of ID. I knew from the beginning that working with them would be like trying to tame wild snakes.

Dealings with these young men had to be treated delicately. Almost all of them had experienced traumatic childhoods. Many had undiagnosed mental health issues, unresolved family problems, and fathers who had been murdered or incarcerated. Quite often, the combined effects of these traumas lead to negative outcomes, including attitudes that rise and fall like the stock market and personalities that can suddenly switch from meek to murderous.

I couldn't turn my back on them. The world had already done so—as it had done in some instances on their fathers and mothers. While I never encouraged or condoned criminal behavior or participated in law-breaking with them, someone in the community had to be their "medicine man" and deal with their sickness without judgment.

Some people, particularly my family, friends, and loved ones, sometimes questioned my sanity, saying it was dangerous or even stupid to help young men like the one I drove to his appointment. However, I have dedicated my life to helping young men just like him. To do so, I must make some very tough decisions and take some calculated risks. This young man had nobody to support him; state institutions and group homes raised him. His mother had been to jail; his father had been killed right in front of him. He had learned his morals and values from killers and convicts. He needed somebody. If I could be a calming influence in his life, it might save society from further tragedy—prevent a murder, robbery, assault, or some other negative outcome.

On that day, the further I drove from his home, the more my anxiety lessened. To calm my spirit, I turned on some soothing gospel music. As I listened to Mahalia Jackson's soul-stirring voice sing "Precious Lord, Take My Hand," I became more peaceful. I drove across the Golden Gate Bridge, thoughtfully staring into the ocean through the downpour of rain splashing against my windshield.

Within half an hour, I was having sushi at an upscale restaurant in beautiful Sausalito, a wealthy community tucked away on the oceanfront across the Golden Gate Bridge about ten minutes from San Francisco—but worlds away from the neighborhood I had just traveled with my young friend. I was meeting with a successful businessman from England who dealt in rare wines and owned several other businesses to talk to him about investing in my new company, Malik Wade Ventures. Before I went inside the restaurant, I sat in the car and reflected on the last two hours of my life. I had gone from riding with an accused killer to sitting in a restaurant with wealthy investors and businessmen.

While I have successfully navigated both worlds on many occasions, this day was especially memorable. It reminded me of the days when I would leave my office in the dangerous Potrero Hill housing projects of San Francisco. Sometimes, seconds after driving away, I could clearly hear gunshots coming from the area I had just left. Less than an hour later, I might be attending a meeting at Stanford Law School, speaking at UC Berkeley, or engaging in a heated discussion with the CEO of a tech company.

I have always embraced this irony. I love the contradiction of it all. Having an office in the projects keeps me grounded. Although it is dangerous, I have learned how to masterfully navigate the landmines and side-step the potential IEDs (improvised explosive devices) of my environment. I've done it most of my life. Both worlds keep me humbled. Big business and academia constantly remind me of the unlimited possibilities of education and industry. Navigating the streets of the inner city, though not in a criminal way, keeps me sharp.

Both are indicative of my unique personality. I don't care to be too polished and puritan-like. That is not my background, and it would be fake and phony if all of a sudden I carried myself like I am some sort of aristocrat. The young men I work with would sniff me out in a second and potentially turn against me. When I meet with millionaire businessmen, I am authentic. I don't over-pronounce my words, although I do speak and express myself clearly. I stay true to myself.

I don't hesitate to be up front with them about my background. Most of the time, they respect my directness and appreciate the fact that I am not hiding anything from them. I am not necessarily trying to be their friend, only commanding respect as a man and giving it in return when warranted. I always humbly express my views, speak my mind, and declare my willingness to work together to create opportunities for young folks in the inner city.

As I left my afternoon business meeting, I had to make another mental adjustment to prepare for a meeting of a different type: politics. The last part of my day was set aside for a conference with a legislative aide who worked with the San Francisco Supervisor's office. I met her at the home she shared with her husband and two small children in a charming neighborhood of million-dollar Victorian homes.

We were meeting to discuss whether she could help eventually purchase a building for my nonprofit organization, Scholastic Interest Group. Since she worked closely at City Hall with individuals who had the power of the purse, including the mayor's office and the Board of Supervisors, she could be very beneficial to me. As I sat in her kitchen, the irony of the situation suddenly struck me. Here I was, sitting in this beautiful home with this couple; he was preparing Italian cuisine while she sipped red wine and their two children received Spanish lessons in a nearby room. The household on the surface seemed picture perfect, and it was a complete contrast from the life that I had lived growing up in the inner city of San Francisco. It was also completely different than many of my current days walking through the trenches of the projects.

After that meeting I went shopping at an organic grocery store called Bi-Rite, located in San Francisco's historic Mission District. The unique store attracts a diverse mixture of ex-hippies and health-food fanatics. The environment was almost cult-like, packed with people who are vegetarians, practice yoga and Pilates, eat tofu and hummus, and meditate and belong to nontraditional spiritual groups. It was another environment that would be incredibly foreign to the kids I work with. I shook my head in disbelief.

As I drove home, I listened to one of my favorite reggae groups, Steele Pulse, and pondered the many facets of my day. All day I had swung from one extreme to another. I replayed the scenes in my mind and smiled: just another day in my new life.

As my mind drifted I couldn't help but wonder what would have happened if I had brought my young friend to my meetings. *Would the second part of my day have gone as smoothly? Would it have been different? Would the businessmen and the legislative aide have embraced me so easily?* This young man had a serious look about him and a noticeable stare; his looks—while normal to me—might have made the patrons of the expensive sushi restaurant do a double take. He might have appeared different and felt out of place in the Victorian home or organic grocery store.

How would the legislative aide's neighbors have reacted if they saw two Black men walking the streets of this quiet neighborhood, especially a young Black man who may outwardly fit the stereotypical description of a thug? I was probably accepted in that area because my attire was similar to that of a schoolteacher, wearing a cardigan sweater and carrying a laptop bag. *But how would my young friend have been received in these different neighborhoods and environments?*

As I drove home I thought about how I could positively influence the views of both groups. I thought about how I could enlighten this young man, change his way of thinking. I had the opportunity to also positively impact the many other young men in the inner city who had similar ways of acting and being—ways that conflicted with many others in the society at large. I don't necessarily think that one way of thinking or belief should rule the other. However, to an extent, the group with the least amount of power and resources has to at least learn to adapt to and respect the laws of society and its systems. If they don't, the answer is obvious: prison.

However, those in power and with wealth have a great responsibility—and a lot to learn—about creating a more equitable and just society that minimizes poverty, makes resources such as housing and jobs available to all, and provides hope to those who are disillusioned and less fortunate. If they could do that, individuals like my young friend would not feel compelled to have a "fuck the world" mentality.

How could I positively influence the wealthy businessmen and patrons in the restaurant to view things differently? To help them understand the plight of people who come from the other side of the tracks? How could I help sway the thinking of the legislative aide who had the power to draft legislation that could ultimately have a beneficial impact on the so-called "least of us?"

As I finally pulled up in front of my home, I sat in the driveway, closed my eyes, meditated silently, and asked myself one profound question: *What could I do to help people understand the ironies of the world?*

30
THE BIRTH OF SOMETHING BEAUTIFUL

Ironically, my quest to address the ironies of the world was born one day in solitary confinement at Taft Correctional Facility in Taft, California in my first year of incarceration. As I lay in my cold, cramped bunk, I thought seriously about what I wanted to do with the rest of my life after I was released. I had been in the hole for a while, and my mind was constantly zigzagging. Although I tried to keep my thoughts optimistic, there were times when I would delve deep into the darkness and become negative. I had to find something positive and constructive to think about or I was going to lose it.

As my thoughts bounced from idea to idea, I realized that I wanted to give back and help rebuild the community that I had helped destroy. If I could start some sort of program that could mentor and teach at-risk youth, then maybe I could inject a bit of positive consciousness into the world and potentially change things for the better. I wanted to plant productive seeds that could be watered and nurtured and eventually grow into a beautiful budding plant that could help my community.

From previous interactions with some of the younger guys in prison, I knew that this would be no easy task. At-risk youth can be difficult to work with, so I would need more than general conversation to attract them. I would have to show them something physical and real. My program would have to be based around a theme such as sports, technology, or hip-hop music or culture. Eventually, I chose sports because they are part of the daily fabric in this country, and most kids, especially those in the inner city, participate in sports as a way to relieve stress or get away from the streets and avoid gangs. I wanted a program that not only taught athletic skills, but also developed character through sports participation.

While in the hole I started to carefully write down my ideas on a tiny piece of paper that I found balled up in the corner of my cell. One of the inmate workers had smuggled me a piece of pencil, and I started eagerly writing my ideas about this program. I wanted to take kids on college tours to places like Howard University and Stanford and bring them guest speakers like Dr. Cornel West, social activist and hip hop artist KRS-One, Dr. Julianne Malveaux, or Professor Michael Eric Dyson. I wanted to help them get internships at technology companies such as Google and Facebook and at law firms. I wanted to take them on trips to Cuba, Egypt, and other unique and fascinating places throughout the world. I wanted to expose them to places, people, and ideas that I never had as a young man. I knew that there was no universal solution for helping at-risk youth, but this could be a start.

I didn't want my program to be just a mainstream sports organization like AAU basketball or Pop Warner football. I wanted something different, something sustainable—an institution that would continue even when I was dead and gone. As I developed my ideas, I learned that nonprofits rely heavily on donations from corporations, organizations, and generous sponsors. Right from the beginning, I bristled at this idea. Since I had been a drug dealer, my natural disposition was entrepreneurial; I believed in doing things for myself and being independent. Consequently, I thought about ways to support my own program and generate revenue to keep it running without having to rely on wealthy folks or institutions outside of the community to sustain it.

When I got out of the hole, I continued to pursue my plan. Other guys on the prison yard would see me cramped up in the corner of the law library, eagerly writing and researching. One day DC, a gang member from Kansas City, strolled over and cynically asked what I was working on.

"A nonprofit for at-risk youth."

He snickered sarcastically. "That ain't gone work; the kids out there don't listen. They are brick headed and can't be reached."

I ignored him and kept writing, but from that moment on, we rarely spoke to each other. I didn't mind losing him as an associate because I didn't appreciate his toxic attitude and subtle attempt to dampen my dream.

The unique mixture of prisoners in federal prisons worked in my favor. On one hand, there were hardcore gang members, dope dealers, and bank robbers. On the other were successful investment bankers, big-time attorneys, and major corporate executives. As I started to write my plan, I sought out some of these brilliant minds to help. I would strategically seek out the formerly successful businessmen to help me proofread my ideas.

I would anxiously await the arrival of certain VIPs who I learned were going to be incarcerated and would immediately approach them and ask for help. Over the years, my plan was edited and rewritten too many times to keep track of. However, by the time my business plan was complete—which was literally days before I got out of prison—it had been proofread by dozens of people, including guys with MBAs and successful entrepreneurs.

I also solicited advice from other street entrepreneurs like myself. Some of the guys from the streets were super shrewd businessmen who had amassed small fortunes in their careers, making millions of dollars in both legal and illegal business ventures. The perspectives of these nontraditional—but still successful—businessmen also proved very helpful.

From day one of my release, I had an intense desire to give back. In my first days of freedom, I burst out the front door of the halfway house to volunteer at a violence prevention program. United Playaz was run by a really good guy with a warm and welcoming spirit, Rudy Corpuz, and was one of the most successful programs in San Francisco. I was able to gain some important experience working with young gang members and hard-to-reach youth. During that time, I also started speaking at schools and the San Francisco Juvenile Hall. Everything started to happen really fast. I couldn't believe that a dream deferred for so many years was finally being realized. I was actually in the community making a difference, simply by sharing my story.

While I was speaking at schools, volunteering my time, and mentoring, I was slowly building my program. I started to scout similar organizations, pulling bits and pieces of information from each to learn what they were doing. Since I had been gone for such a long time, I had to do my homework on the current best practices. Things had changed, and youngsters were a lot different. They were totally consumed with social media, video games, iPhones, and so on. Making matters worse, way too many of them were also ambitious to be ruthless killers, robbers, and representatives of their neighborhoods in beefs. Unfortunately, this was the new normal in the hood.

I continued to rebuild my reputation in the community, this time as a do-gooder and someone who gives back rather than takes. My résumé was improving by the day! In the meantime, my plan was further refined by my time in Stanford University's Project ReMADE. Given all this progress, after about a year I felt ready to hit the streets full time and really make a difference.

Scholastic Interest Group (SIG) is the nonprofit organization born from my years of planning and preparation. SIG is a mentoring program for at-risk student athletes in San Francisco that uses sports and education as vehicles to teach character development, community service, college preparation, and career readiness.

SIG started simple. I would take a few local kids to the community park or rec center and do exercises with them. We would run wind sprints, do burpees and push-ups, or have an intense basketball workout. Initially, I started with a small group I could easily enroll: kids whose parents I had grown up with. The first group consisted of young men like Geru and Lajarie Mabrey, Deandre Otis, Jamar Shepard, Shaquile Cooper, and Ricky Johnson. While they did not initially know it, this small group was the birth of SIG. They were the beginning of an institution.

Before we worked out, I would always give the kids a lesson or a word for the day. We would talk about character development, African American history, politics, current events, and discipline. At first, they weren't comfortable with these types of discussions because they weren't used to being talked to like this. Most of their coaches simply taught them about basketball or football but didn't stress the tools and life skills they would need to navigate society as young Black men.

When it came time to recruit kids so that I could expand SIG, I went back to my old neighborhood, specifically to the three remaining primarily Black communities in San Francisco: Bayview Hunters Point, the Fillmore District, and Visitation Valley. Initially, I was not well-received—the neighborhood attitude toward me was even cold at times. I didn't get offended or discouraged, but my feelings were bruised a bit. I couldn't understand why the kids and their parents would not be responsive to someone wanting to help them. *All I want to do is make a difference.*

Some of the parents were obvious in their suspicions and skepticism and told me so point blank. Over time, I started to understand that the parents and kids had every right to be suspicious of me. I had been away from the community for decades, and parents had no proof that I was not a sick psychopath or pedophile who preyed on children. Ultimately and understandably, parents have a duty to protect their most prized possessions. Quite honestly, I agree that anyone who works with children should be thoroughly screened and scrutinized—I was no exception.

The kids themselves were also understandably standoffish. They were young teenagers. I had been in prison for most of their lives, so they were naturally hesitant to open up and trust me. Many of the kids had no fathers, so they were already suffering from abandonment issues and trust issues. Many others were traumatized for a slew of other reasons as well.

To lessen the community concerns, I made it a point to be completely clear and upfront about my background. I became highly visible at AAU basketball and Pop Warner and high school football games, schools, churches, and community centers. I openly engaged the community and offered media interviews. I enthusiastically introduced parents and children to my fiancée and showed them where I lived and where my grandmother had lived for over fifty years. I introduced some of them to my mother and sisters. I wanted to eliminate any doubts about my motives.

Over time, the tension started to finally diminish, and parents started to actually seek me out to request that I mentor their sons. As time went on, several fathers in the community asked that I not only provide physical conditioning workouts for their sons, but to mentor them as well, in order to reinforce their positions as fathers. It felt good that my time and effort was beginning to pay off.

Eventually, young kids and teenagers would swarm me almost anywhere I walked in San Francisco.

"Hey Brother Malik, I am on the honor roll. Thank you for motivating me."

"I am off of probation now; thanks for coming to court."

"I read that book that you gave me."

I would grin, maybe give them a heartfelt hug or handshake, and walk away feeling good. My long deferred dream was starting to pay dividends.

There are many SIG stories I am proud of, but two in particular stick out to me. One is the story of Jayvon "Hitz" who grew up in the Valencia Gardens housing projects in San Francisco. I met him when I spoke at San Francisco Juvenile Hall. Jayvon, who had a dangerous reputation, had already been shot in the back and was currently in Juvenile Hall for a violent gun-related charge.

He had participated in a discussion group that I was facilitating, and I immediately noticed that he was different from the others. He was reading a book when he walked into the classroom, and he asked me thought-provoking questions, took notes, and had a serious look in his eyes during my talk. Jayvon was determined to learn. When the session was over, we talked one-on-one, and he expressed his sincere desire to change.

Jayvon said he admired how I spoke and expressed myself and asked me how I built up my vocabulary. He asked me to recommend some books, so I told him to first start with the dictionary and thesaurus. Then I recommended a few books such as *The Autobiography of Malcolm X, Manchild in the Promised Land* by Claude Brown, and Michelle Alexander's *The New Jim Crow*. I also told him to read the *San Francisco Chronicle* every day.

Several months later, I ran into Jayvon at a fast-food restaurant in Daly City. We embraced and shared what was going on in our lives. He told me he had been out for several months and was doing well. He had enrolled in Skyline Community College and was mentoring kids in his old neighborhood in the Gardens. He had also started doing some freelance photography and videography work. I told him I was very proud of him and hoped he'd stay in touch.

It pleased me to know he could quote word for word many of the things I discussed with him at Juvenile Hall. It was obvious that what I said had some impact on him. He was a shining example of what I wanted to accomplish with SIG. Jayvon was the physical manifestation of my vision while I sat in the filthy hole in prison.

I am also particularly proud of my relationship with a young man named Jamar who I have worked with for a couple of years. Jamar's family comes from a rough area of San Francisco called the Army Street projects. In 2015 Jamar's fourteen-year-old cousin was senselessly stabbed to death by a gang member; the loss of his younger cousin nearly sent Jamar over the edge. However, Jamar eventually regained focus with school and football; instead of avenging his younger cousin's death, he stayed on course and accepted a scholarship to play football at San Jose State.

Young men like Jamar make all my efforts worth it. When I see a young man go off to college, get an internship at a law firm, or go from an F student to an A student, it warms me inside. That is why I do what I do. Not for any personal accolades or accomplishments, but to give others hope and inspiration.

Countless young men have told me how one of my speeches or a mentoring session I had with them profoundly impacted their lives. The stories of young men like Jamar and Jayvon motivate and inspire me when I promote SIG to millionaire venture capitalists and successful CEOs, when I accept large checks from individuals or businesses, or when I speak at Cal Berkeley or San Francisco State. The kids are my rallying cry. They are my fight song. They are the "five smooth stones and a slingshot" that I use to slay Goliath.

Ultimately, I want SIG to be an institution that will leave a legacy long after I am gone. I want SIG to own and acquire property that students and their offspring can always call their own—that they can build upon literally and figuratively. Today

I run SIG from the beautiful confines of the Bayview YMCA, a state-of-the-art building in the community where I grew up and live today—not from the crummy confines of the prison cell where I first dreamed of such an organization.

It all started as a dream deferred, but now it is a dream realized.

31
COLLEGE BOUND

My stomach stirs with butterflies. I'm as nervous as a freshman on the first day of high school. It's finally here! I have dreamed of this day for many years. Today I am taking fifteen kids on an all-expenses-paid tour of UCLA, University of Southern California, Pepperdine University, Loyola Marymount, and Cal State Northridge.

This trip has the potential to be life-changing for them—and me. Some of these kids have never been on a plane before; some have not even traveled out of their neighborhoods. This trip can open them up and stimulate their senses.

As we prepare to board the van heading to the airport, the kids are running around with unfiltered nervous energy and laughter. The young men clown around and horseplay, perform silly dances, give each other high fives, and tease each other. The proud parents watch, beaming with delight. I unsuccessfully try to conceal my own excitement; I am usually straight-faced but today I hang loose and act a little silly with the kids. Instead of going into my usual army drill sergeant routine, I allow myself to lighten up a little and let them have a bit of fun. I don't typically like a lot of pictures but, caught up in the merriment of the moment, I flash a huge Kool-Aid smile for the cameras.

Beneath the high-energy hijinks, I sense a hint of uneasiness in a couple of the parents. They are sending their children far away for the first time with someone they have only known a short time; they are putting complete trust in me to return their children safe and unharmed. I don't take their uneasiness personally but try to kindly reassure them. As we board the van, I give the parents and guardians reaffirming hugs and handshakes to let them know it's all good.

As we drive to the airport, I keep a cool and in-command demeanor; internally, though, I'm experiencing a bit of tension as my thoughts periodically flash back to my life of selling drugs. During my drug career, I would often be in deep thought as I headed to the airport en route to one of my drug operations. I would be mentally visualizing different dangerous scenarios, exit strategies, and back-up plans to deflect the Feds, the killers, and the kidnappers. Once at the airport, I would behave as low-key as possible, moving discreetly, wiggling through the airport while mentally preparing myself for the worst, knowing that the Feds could be monitoring my every movement.

This time, it is obviously different. I don't have to worry about the DEA, customs agents, or the FBI abruptly detaining me, wanting to pat me down and search my baggage. Even so, although I no longer sell drugs, the fear and dread of law enforcement and a phobia about airports stay with me. Walking through the airport on this day with this group of young men, I feel a pinch of paranoia. I still suffer from the residual effects of being a drug dealer. Sadly, some things never leave . . .

All eyes are on my group as we walk through the airport terminal. We are eye-catching. All seventeen of us, including a chaperone and me, are uniformed with special sweatshirts custom-made with the SIG logo. For the moment, we move like the Marines, conducting ourselves as a cohesive organized unit. As we board the plane, I pause for a split second and look around in wonder, contemplating my amazement at it all. Years ago, I was flying to LA to do a drug deal that could have landed me in prison for the rest of my life. Today, I am giving life by giving hope to future generations of scholars and leaders in the inner city.

A few hours later, we are at Pepperdine University, a breathtaking, postcard-worthy college campus in the wealthy enclave of Malibu. The campus looks more like a five-star resort in Cancun, Mexico, than a college campus. It is absolutely mind-blowing. When we first arrive, we pause and stand on a steep hillside at the peak of the campus and gaze at endless miles of ocean.

As I stand there with the young men, I feel like a proud father; they snap pictures and play in the grass. I simply inhale the beauty of the campus—and these kids. The moment is exciting beyond explanation. This very moment is the pinnacle of everything that I had dreamed of while locked up. To give these young men this opportunity, I wouldn't change anything about my life—not even my time in prison.

> I am especially moved when one of the kids pulls me to the side and expresses his appreciation for the opportunity. He says he never dreamed that he would be visiting a college campus.

After we left Pepperdine, I took the young men to eat at world-famous Roscoe's House of Chicken and Waffles. Roscoe's is an LA landmark known for its great food and celebrity visitors—President Barack Obama and rapper Snoop Dogg among them. I wanted them to be able to tell their friends and family back home that they had eaten there among LA's stars and famous folks. Such experiences can go a long way in terms of planting positive seeds for the future for inner-city kids by making them feel worthy to experience life outside of the hood.

The next day we visited the spectacular campus of the University of Southern California (USC). As we toured the university, we got lucky and were able to catch a football workout with former USC Trojan and NFL Jacksonville Jaguar receiver Marqise Lee. After the workout, Marqise was generous enough to talk to the young men, emphasizing the importance of academics and hard work as they listened with rapt attention. I stood there firmly relishing the moment like a concerned father figure. This is what it is all about: exposure, stimulation, and opportunity.

It is my hope that this trip, along with similar moments and opportunities SIG can provide in the future, will motivate these young men to achieve, to dream, to conquer and accomplish their goals, big and small. I pray that twenty years from now—when some of them are schoolteachers and architects and business owners—they will say that this moment was instrumental in helping them realize that they could be whatever they wanted in life.

This trip, we hit some major schools in Southern California; next, maybe we will be touring Harvard or a historical Black college or university; then perhaps the University of South Africa. As it turns out, I will be taking a couple of them to the University of Ghana in March 2017. Without education there is no foundation.

I want to be a small part of their solution. When all is said and done and my life is over, I want to have been thoroughly used up by the youth in my community. I want to use every bit of my being to be a protector and provider for them and my community—not a parasite as I was in my prior life. Things have to come full circle.

Organizing the trip was hard work. But with lots of help from SIG's board of directors, I was able to get the trip fully sponsored by small foundations and individuals. There was no cost to the participants. It was very expensive to foot the bill for seventeen plane flights, hotels, food, etc. But I was determined. I didn't take no for an answer. I strongly feel that the supposed "least of us" deserve the chance to be exposed to a college tour. I feel compelled to provide these young men with a fighting chance. No matter what, I will make it happen for them. I must give them the exposure that I didn't get as a young Black boy. Such exposure could have afforded me the opportunity to be great in something other than dealing dope.

As we fly back home, soaring 20,000 feet in the sky, I stare out of my window and gaze into the clouds, reflecting on the past few days. I think about those magnificent college campuses. I picture the spontaneous smiles on the faces of the young men; I reminisce about the kids budding and blooming right before my eyes into mature young men.

But I worry, too. Is a college tour enough? What else do they need as young Black males to survive? What else can either SIG or I do to arm them for the their future? What other opportunities do they need that I can provide? If not me, then who? If not now, then when?

32
I CAN BREATHE

Tuesday October 20, 2015
Sweat forms on my forehead and in my armpits. The back of my neck and the collar of my shirt are drenched as I zigzag in and out of traffic, honking at the snail drivers. I grit my teeth as I punch the gas pedal. I have to be in court in ten minutes.

My life hinges on the flow of traffic. Damn, there is an accident up ahead on the 101 Freeway. I manage to wiggle through the traffic to my exit, park in the first place I can find, and make a mad dash to the courthouse, which is about three blocks away. *Shit! I have to see the judge in six minutes!*

My phone rings but I can't break stride, so I don't answer. When I stop to catch my breath, I see that the missed phone call was from an unidentified number. Probably my attorney calling to ask where I am. I curse myself under my breath for being late.

I am rarely late for anything. How could I be late for one of the most important days in the last twenty-three years of my life? I stride into the courtroom at 11 a.m. on the button—right on time. As I walk in, obviously sweating and breathing a little heavily, all eyes in the courtroom turn my direction and the hushed conversation in the room abruptly stops. My lawyer shoots me a cutting look, as if to say, "*Where the hell have you been?*"

It's a creepy feeling walking into a federal courtroom again after so many years. The last time I was in a courthouse I was handed a fourteen-year federal prison sentence. But today I am here petitioning the court to release me from federal supervision and terminate the remaining two years of my sentence—something they rarely do.

The last twenty-three years have been a never-ending bad dream. It's possible that dream could end today, that I could remove myself from the vise grips of the federal government. It's been three years since I was released from prison. Since that time, I have demonstrated undeniable change for the better and have never violated my probation or tested positive for drugs or alcohol.

As I walk to the podium to face the judge, I am confident. I feel as if I am playing in the Super Bowl and winning by two touchdowns going into the fourth quarter. I know that my post-release résumé is impressive. But when dealing with the Feds, anything can happen, so I also remain humble.

Even though I'm confident, it is still nerve-racking to walk into a huge, echoing federal courtroom. The Brazilian cherrywood walls subtly imply power and a sense of supremacy. The high-vaulted ceilings seem to rise endlessly into the sky, signifying the unlimited power and authority of the federal government.

Although I am focused and determined to win the case, I refrain from being cocky or overconfident. I completely understand that I am still the visitor—the underdog trying to beat the champion. I am on the government's home field, and it is one (me) against nine: three probation officers, three district attorneys, two United States Marshals, and the judge. Although many of the officers and attorneys aren't connected to my case directly, their mere presence in the courtroom is a strategic show of force. It is a subtle tactic intended to remind me: *You are in our house.*

My gray slacks, gray sweater, and black dress shoes are professional and conservative—more suitable for a stockbroker on Wall Street than a federal felon. In choosing my attire for the day, I specifically wanted to demonstrate my transformation from a twenty-one-year-old, unrepentant drug dealer wearing flashy clothing and a diamond-crusted Rolex to a forty-four-year-old, professional-looking executive director of a nonprofit with a purpose in life.

As I walk to the podium, I glimpse something in my peripheral vision and unintentionally lock eyes with one of the federal probation officers, a man named Magana. We engage in a brief staring match, and I can feel his contempt. Magana has a big reputation among former inmates as an arrogant asshole who wants to send guys straight back to prison. In actuality he shouldn't be here; I'm not on his caseload. He is attending the hearing for one reason: to intimidate me. From a distance, we stand nose-to-nose.

Senior Judge Susan Ilston has a calm demeanor, and she doesn't try to scare me or use her bully pulpit to force me into submission or to surrender. She clearly sees that I am no longer the twenty-one-year-old, desensitized drug dealer who once preyed on the community. When she speaks, she praises my accomplishments, complimenting me for the work I've done in the community and as a mentor to other former inmates now on federal probation.

My probation officer smiles faintly and is fairly friendly on this day, making positive comments on my behalf and portraying me as the perfect client. They share nothing but compliments about me. A member of the U.S. Attorney's Office says his office sees few cases that warrant early release but agrees that mine is a compelling case. There are no arguments made against my motion to be granted early release. In the end, Judge Ilston congratulates me and wishes me luck.

And *poof!* Just like magic, I have my life back. Words can't accurately explain how it feels to have the heavy foot of the federal government finally off my neck.

As I walked out of the courtroom a free man, I smiled broadly and spoke to everyone I passed: the doorman, the hobo on the street, and even the guy in the car who almost hit me in the crosswalk at the stoplight. I must have smiled at everyone in sight. I stopped the first person I saw and asked them to take a picture of me right in front of the federal building in my new essence as a free man. I wasn't gloating or taking a victory lap, only capturing the moment.

I immediately drove about twenty minutes to Oakland so I could dine at world-famous Everett and Jones Barbecue. I ordered one of my favorite meals: sliced barbecue, macaroni and cheese, potato salad, and ice cold lemonade. The food seemed to taste even better than usual; my newfound freedom must have been stimulating my taste buds!

As I savored my food, I started to reminisce about the last three years in which I had to confront the realities of being a federal felon. It had been a very long road, but my difficult journey had given me perspective. I learned that I didn't know it all when I was a drug dealer with a lot of money and a lot of material possessions. I had to learn when to shut up, humble myself, and listen to wise counsel. I learned just how powerful the government was, but ultimately—and more importantly—I learned just how powerful I was in transforming my own thinking in a positive way.

It had been humbling to discover that I wasn't as smart as I thought I was when I was twenty-one. And I agreed with the proverb made famous by the Greek philosopher Socrates, that says, "I knew nothing." The more I learned, the more I found out just how tiny I was in the big picture of knowledge and the universe.

From the beginning of my journey, I had a very strategic plan to transcend and overcome my situation—to navigate prison and to get off supervised release early. There was always a method to my madness. For the next phase of my life, I also have plans: a five-year plan, a ten-year plan, and a twenty-year plan, all of them specific and focused. These plans came as a result of careful preparation while in prison.

Being completely free of federal restraints meant I could smile freely and not have to worry that some coldhearted convicts will think I'm soft because I'm trying to be human and compassionate rather than animalistic. I could finally shed some of the armor I have been wearing for over two decades because I won't have to appear to be an unbreakable warrior 24/7. I began to lower the defense mechanisms I had used for so many years in order to survive spiritually, emotionally, and mentally.

I rejoiced that I could freely exercise my inner nerd, the geeky bookworm hidden deep inside my soul. I could let people in; I could open up and be less tense. However, I knew all these changes would not happen overnight. I was determined not to force it but to let it happen naturally. I knew it would come bit by bit as I hiked the beautiful mountains of Mount Tamalpais in Marin County, as I walked barefoot at Ocean Beach, and rode my bike in Golden Gate Park. It would come as I engaged in things that allowed me to truly be a free spirit, unrestrained by the federal government or of the false limitations I had placed on myself for the past two decades. Now I would finally be free from those false barriers.

At the restaurant, I thought about what I had lost over the years. The lingering effects are devastating, but they can be reversed by prayer, meditation, and being honest with myself. Some things may be lost forever. Those are the facts. I entered prison in my twenties and returned to society in my forties; I can't recapture that time. However, I can make my years to come count for something.

I determined to make peace with the negative legacy of my past. I believe the more good works that I do, the more people will let the past fade into the background.

I had a pretty good résumé to build on by the day I earned my early release, and I anticipated things only getting better. There will be larger venues at which to speak, bigger programs to run to reach more kids and change more young lives. In the past I had been asked to speak in many different places throughout the world, including the Philippines and other parts of Asia, but I could never accept those invitations because I was still on probation. From that day forward, I could move ahead without the rigid restrictions of the federal government delaying me from my accomplishments.

Now, the sky is the limit.

My Federal register number, 09393–041, is a thing of the past. It's dead and buried. For many years, as far as the Feds were concerned, I was only a case file, and I didn't have any say in my life, my fate, or my destiny. I was at the complete mercy of the government. Starting today, the only person who can stop me is me. There are no limitations. Instead of just daydreaming, reading books, and hearing from others about their experiences, I can now actually travel to Cuba, Africa, Brazil, and other places throughout the globe. As I move forward, I truly plan to make the rest of my life the best of my life.

33
THE POWER OF LISTENING

One simple but practical solution to many pressing problems we face in society today, particularly those related to our youth, is for adults to simply *listen,* and to pay closer attention as young people make clumsy and sometimes difficult-to-understand pleas for help. If we're not listening and not paying close attention, we may misunderstand their pleas for help and misinterpret their petitions for attention as deviant or defiant behaviors.

As a young man, I desperately cried out for help, but few people took heed. If they did, they didn't act aggressively on what they heard. I symbolically hollered for help when I started selling crack at the age of fifteen, and when I packed a pistol to Jefferson High School at age sixteen. There had to be some adult somewhere who saw me getting off the tracks and slipping away. Was there no adult in my everyday environment who could successfully pull my coattail?

Growing up, I had a nosy neighbor named Margie who saw me nearly every day, she would give me "the eye," which said, *Boy, you better watch it.* She made subtle comments about what I was doing with my life. However, although she gave good advice and I knew that she loved me, she was participating in some of the exact activity that she was warning me against. This ultimately just left me confused.

I badly needed a mentor to help guide me and to offer some insight into life's riddles. I needed someone to monitor and track me in school as well as socially. Though I was a good student, an extra push might have allowed me to go from a 3.0 to a 4.0 grade point average. Although education alone is no cure-all, it could have possibly kept me on track.

Beyond education, mentoring and motivation from my "village" could have helped me get involved with positive programs other than sports, such as creative writing classes, book clubs, and chess clubs—things that I naturally lean toward and which could have served me very well. As research has indicated over and over again, the more time young folks spend in positive activities, the less time that they have to get in trouble.

In the Black community, the women—especially the grandmothers—are typically the soothsayers and providers of insight. Although God sees everything, it seems like grandmothers see everything, too. They have a mysterious intuitive ability that sometimes seems psychic, allowing them to predict the future with pinpoint accuracy. Listen to Grandma!

My mother did her best raising a young man-child alone. It was truly a struggle considering that I was over six feet tall by the time I was thirteen and physically towered over her. I was also able to trick and mischievously manipulate her and was very careful to hide my dishonorable deeds from her. She knew that I wasn't a Boy Scout, so to speak, but her awareness of the extent of my criminal activity was limited. She was too busy working very hard, as an administrative assistant for Kaiser hospital commuting several hours to and from work every day, singlehandedly raising my two siblings and me. She was just too exhausted and burned out to thoroughly investigate any suspicions she might have had about me. At home, I was quiet and low-key, and she knew I was a good student and athlete. When I left the house, however, I transformed into a sneaky drug dealer.

Ultimately, it is the community's collective responsibility to keep a keen eye peeled for kids who have natural talents and gifts and for those who are expressing subtle signs of wanting or needing help. When kids act out and join gangs, commit crime, become sexually promiscuous, or use drugs, they are screaming *Help!* Screaming for the attention and affection of not just their parents, but of any caring adult.

As adults, we must be proactive and assertive about sideways behavior by our youth and be on the lookout for certain warning signs in the young people we come in contact with and care about. We must use our abilities of discernment to look past the sagging pants and sometimes hard-to-understand mannerisms. We must attentively listen to the messages in the lyrics of rap and other music popular with young people to see how we can use them as teaching tools. And we must listen to the pain that youth may be expressing in the music itself. We must overlook the rough and rugged disguise of young folks who outwardly look like thugs. We must consider the possibility that dreadlocks and braids, gold teeth, tattoos, and piercings are forms of creative and sometimes cultural expression. Working to understand our own perspectives can ultimately allow us to unearth the beauty that lies within every child. We shouldn't *judge* our children; we should *hug* our children.

Sadly, today, too many kids don't feel loved. They feel that adults are cold, condescending, and only want to talk *at* them rather than *to* them. They feel that we only want to impose our will and ideas on them—push them around with our authority and enforce our "adultist" views—rather than facilitating a process that allows them to feel heard.

Immediate changes in the attitudes of our youth could be sparked if more adults took just one moment to talk to a child and ask them a few simple questions: *Who are you? What is your purpose in life?* Imagine large groups of compassionate, caring adults and mentors in each community nurturing kids who aren't their own—taking them to dinner at a decent restaurant or engaging in some other positive activity with them. Symbolically, this represents an ideal world at its most minute yet significant level.

As parents, mentors, teachers, and "chiefs of the village," our efforts have to be sustained and consistent. Kids—particularly kids in the inner city—have issues with abandonment, rejection, and trust; therefore, efforts to connect with them must be unshakable. This advice doesn't apply only to kids in the inner city, however. Kids want and need attention whether they live in the suburbs, small towns, or rural areas; whether their families are rich, poor, or somewhere in between. Many kids from all sectors of society in our country are disillusioned and disconnected from their parents and could benefit from mentors or other adults who will truly pay attention to them.

I was fortunate to have a couple of different men in my life who paid some attention to me and made me feel important and loved; their efforts at least partially offset the negative impact of my inconsistent relationship with my father and stepfather. One man who had an impact on me was Manuel Moreno. His son Jesse was one of my best friends growing up, and we played on the same basketball team at Epiphany Catholic School when I was eleven. Manuel was a good man—a tough, old-school Mexican dude. He was strong, smart, and very masculine, which I respected.

Manuel was the first person to ever take me to a restaurant for a meal—the Peppermill Restaurant in Daly City, where I ordered buffalo wings and nachos. I still remember that meal, and I still like to eat out at restaurants today. However, once Jesse and I lost contact, my relationship with Manuel faded as well. I don't fault Mr. Moreno, and I am grateful for his mentorship, but as a rule we have to be consistent in the lives of our young people. In many cases, relationships like this can turn out to be counterproductive, as they heighten a young person's feelings of abandonment and make it harder for them to trust adults.

It sounds cliché, but in regards to our youth, love is the most universal answer. The benefits of showing love are real and can reap immediate rewards. Youth who come from challenged backgrounds—particularly kids with low self-esteem, kids in juvenile hall or foster homes, or kids with special needs—react especially positively to being shown love.

To make a serious change in the world, we need a massive mentor movement now. Adults with the heart, time, and energy can start where we are, with whatever we have, and try to make a positive impact on a young person's life. It could be a nephew or niece or the child of a close friend who needs somebody in his or her life. You don't need any special qualifications to do this. You don't have to be rich, have a college degree, or come from a particular background; the only requirement is that you sincerely want to help young folks.

Everything I have experienced in my life has prepared me to mentor and help kids. The many days and nights of cautiously peeking out the window looking for the Feds make me want to prevent any other young person from ever experiencing that type of trauma. I don't want any young person to ever have to go through the tension I endured when rival factions squared off in the prison yard getting ready to fight to the death. In prison, I tossed and turned anxiously many nights after reading a newspaper report of gang violence or a senseless murder because I knew there were young folks out there who needed someone like me to genuinely care about their well-being.

Who better to distribute this information than someone like me who has survived the purgatory of prison and returned like Daniel from the lion's den? Men like me, who have experienced much of the good and bad that life has to offer, can make a huge impact on society, whether we have done time in prison or not. Are there enough of us foot soldiers who want to stand on the front line?

This is my confrontational call to action. Where are the strong warriors and battle-tested men in the community? Where are the intellectuals and the thinkers? Where are those who, like myself, used to be five-star generals for Satan? Those who previously helped promote evil and wrongdoing? What is stopping us from taking back the hearts and minds of our young people? What is preventing me from having more of an impact? I can do more. I should do more. I *must* do more!

These days I can be found regularly at juvenile court; at San Francisco City Hall when legislation concerning our children is being considered; at high school and junior high school football and basketball games cheering for the players. I am in the alleyways of the projects and on the block. I am in the hood wearing my black hoodie in solidarity with the youth while trying to give them a voice. We need all hands on deck.

And we also need financial support. Only some of us are both willing *and* able to roll up our sleeves at 5 a.m. on a daily basis to interrupt the patterns we see among our youth. There are other means of supporting, however, and those who can't contribute with time can contribute through donations. I want to be more than a chronic complainer about the sagging pants, the music, and the disrespect for authority by our youth, and I invite you to take action in the ways that make sense for you.

We have to make our presence felt in the lives of the youth. We can't be shrinking violets. We cannot be passive when we see youth acting out at school, in public, or on the bus. I have learned a subtle science to approaching youth when they are misbehaving, and it seems to work nearly every time. I have engaged the most disrespectful youth from various backgrounds and cultures with love and compassion, and it works. I will often sympathetically approach a young person on the bus, at school, or in public if I hear them using destructive language or demonstrating disregard for the feelings of others, and I will very humbly bring their conduct to their attention. To this day, I have never been disrespected by a young person when I have approached them in this way. I come at them "correct," as they say in the streets. I have approached young men with pistols bulging from their waists and calmly and humbly tried to get them to think about their behavior. I don't approach them arrogantly or condescendingly because that could be deadly. I approach them peacefully with intense compassion in my eyes. The simplicity of this method is striking. I hedge my bet with humility.

To be clear, folks should have some level of operational understanding about the community if they plan to employ this tactic. You must be at least somewhat culturally competent to minimize the chance that this tactic will backfire. In fact, if you're not from the community, approaching a young person in this way can be downright risky.

One of the best ways to reach young people is to take them out of their immediate environment, preferably out in the wilderness or on a college campus tour—away from the gangs and the hustle and bustle of the city, and away from their iPhones, Instagram, and Snapchat accounts. Away from the music, the mind-numbing weed that many of them smoke, the cough syrup some of them sip, and the prescription pills that some of them may pop.

I have done this on a small level by simply taking kids out of their neighborhood to eat lunch. Most times, they completely transform from gun-toting gang members to quiet kids who read and recite poetry. They transform into their authentic selves; they switch from G-Force the gang member to Gregory the poet. They do this when they can relax and not have to watch their backs or "put on." If this experience can be replicated and done on a consistent basis on a bigger platform, we could have a winning model—a system that could have far-reaching impact. Imagine the impact on our country if Shaquille O'Neal, Jay Z, or Oprah sponsored and supported highly publicized, sustainable, national mentoring programs.

We are at a critical juncture in society today, and, unfortunately, we are letting music, the Internet, and social media mentor and guide our kids. We must aggressively snatch back control. If we do not, the U.S. will continue to be ranked fourteenth in the world in education and first in the world for incarceration. If we don't take action, the cancer of gangs and violence will continue to metastasize and grow out of control. Our children will leave home in the morning and return at night unrecognizable. Right in front of our eyes, they will grotesquely mutate as their speech and actions become unrecognizable. By then it will be too late. They will have become Frankenstein's monster.

I believe kids everywhere in the world—not just in the U.S.—should have mentors and sufficient resources. I believe we all can do better jobs of investing our time and our money in our most precious resource: our children.

I don't think we can wait for government to solve this problem. We must act now regardless of government measures.

I think each one can teach one. Today, we can all shake the hand of a young man or woman, meet them where they are, and simply ask, "How can I help you?"

34
AN OPEN LETTER TO MY COMMUNITY

Dear community,

    I hope this letter finds you well.

    I'm writing to apologize for the hurt and pain that I have caused you. I feel that I owe you a personal apology for my actions over the past thirty years. I know it has been extremely difficult for you, and I am truly sorry that you had to suffer at the hands of my poor decision-making.

    After you finish reading this letter, I hope that you will be able to forgive me, as I have a tremendous amount of respect and love for you, and I feel compelled to clearly explain my position. This is my confession.

    Part of the reason the community is in such confusion and chaos today is because of the damage done by drugs being sold in the community. When I drive around my neighborhood today and I see people wandering the streets talking to themselves, eating food out of the garbage can, strung out, or lacking all hope due to drug use, I can't help but ask myself what role I played in the tragedy at hand.

When someone has been shot, maimed, or otherwise badly hurt, I ask myself, *Are my hands indirectly stained with their blood?* These are hard but necessary questions to ask myself. I apologize to the many mothers who have lost their sons in the streets to senseless violence that may have been connected to drug activity I initiated.

Drugs destroy lives. Even though I never used drugs, they destroyed my life, deeply affected the lives of my family members, and devastated the entire community. I am not proud of having uncaringly sold drugs to friends and close relatives—people I claimed to love. I preyed on their weaknesses for my own monetary gain so that I could drive a new Mercedes Benz or wear a fancy diamond-crusted Rolex. The Mercedes Benz was bought with blood money, and the watch was worn with wretchedness attached to it.

As a side effect of drugs being sold—by myself and others—in my community, we now have a huge group of young men with no sense of guidance and direction. Many are totally disrespectful to adults and all authority figures. They see no way out other than to sling dope in the hood, gangbang, or hang on the block with pistols hugging their hips. Many of them have fathers who are in prison, strung out on drugs, or forever damaged by the many years of drug abuse that caused them to completely give up on life.

Today, the drug that I sold, crack cocaine, is not as popular as it once was on the streets. However, as a result of crack cocaine bulldozing the pathway, the preferred drugs of choice today are meth—also known as "crystal"—Ecstasy, prescription pills like

Xanax and OxyContin, and cough syrup, known on the streets as "lean."

Although I share the blame with many culprits, conspirators, and others who have been complicit in this widespread tragedy resulting in the drastic demise of the community, I take responsibility for my personal role in this catastrophe.

I grew up during the widespread crack epidemic of the '80s. I was one of thousands of primarily young Black and Latino men in the inner cities of America, from San Francisco to St. Louis, who mistakenly sought stardom and celebrity through drug sales. However, I was always slightly different than many of my peers, as I was somewhat conscious of my actions; I can't use the excuse that I didn't know better—because I did.

In the back of my mind, I had an idea of the poisonous nature of drugs and how they affect the community. The negative impact was clear to me when I saw the crack babies hysterically hollering and crying from hunger, wearing filthy diapers, their noses oozing with snot while their mothers left them unattended and desperately hit the crack pipe. It was real to me as I watched some of the women in my community sell their bodies for five dollars just to get a hit and as I saw young men in my community gunned down in cold blood.

Today when I see a drug addict drifting through the street, it is an immediate trigger for me—a fleeting moment when the negative nostalgia leaps to the front of my mind. I can vividly remember walking into a crack house when I was around fifteen and selling a mother some crack as her babies screamed at the top of their lungs while their mother fidgeted and fumbled for loose change to get a hit. As I walked in the house, the stench was like a punch to the face. It was like visiting a trash dump. Dirty underwear lay on the living room carpet, which was pitch black—as if someone changed car oil on it. Mice darted across the floor, while roaches crawled the kitchen countertops. I can never forget how I stood there, casually spitting sunflower seeds on the floor, looking at this mother with disgust while she frenetically searched her tattered purse for change. I can never forget how she picked scabs on her face and convulsed—her body seeming to move without her permission—all side effects of being a dope fiend.

I am ashamed when I think of that moment and the funky smell of that house and that mother's sense of desperation as she frantically searched the crevices of the couch for loose change.

I apologize to that women and to her children. I hope they are okay today, despite the odds. I hope her son didn't grow up to be a cold-blooded killer because of the trauma and anger he might have harbored because his mother was a dope fiend. I hope her daughter didn't grow up to sell her precious body for five dollars to feel loved. I hope they somehow managed to beat the odds and become something better than their mother and me.

Today, I want to help young people. I know young folks have brilliant, original, and exciting ideas and many of the answers to life's puzzles. They can conquer the world. They are smart and intuitive and just need to be given a chance. I want to help give them a chance. I believe at this stage in my life I have something valuable to offer them: possible insight into their future.

While I direct my apology to anyone who may have been affected directly or indirectly by my actions, I want to focus especially on the cities of San Francisco, New York, Washington, D.C., Pittsburgh, Minneapolis, Louisville, Seattle, Tacoma, Los Angeles, and Indianapolis. These are all places where I directly contaminated the soil by bringing negative energy and bad karma to the environment.

I will never fully know the trail of ruin that I left behind in those cities, but I can use my imagination, which often softly tugs at my conscience. I do know that twenty-five years later, every one of those cities has a horrifying gang problem; each of them has a significant prison population; and in each of them, many lives have been lost and/or destroyed because of their drug trades.

I express deep empathy for the young men I met while in prison who are serving ridiculously long sentences. I apologize to the nineteen-year-old man I met who was serving 120 years for selling crack. He grew up without a father and was raised in the notorious Cabrini-Green projects on the South Side of Chicago by a drug-addicted mother.

I apologize to the mothers and grandmothers who would give me mean stares and dirty looks of disapproval as I stood in their neighborhoods and sold crack with no remorse or regrets. I am not proud of having offended them or making them feel fearful. Nobody should be a prisoner in their own home.

I ask for forgiveness from my mother for the pain that she experienced visiting me in juvenile hall, coming to see me in federal prison, and having her front door kicked down and her house raided by the police searching for drugs. I apologize for the worry and anxiety she experienced as a result of me being on the FBI's wanted list for years, while she hoped and prayed that they wouldn't shoot and kill her only son while trying to catch me.

I say sorry to the young men I left to fend for themselves in the community. Every community needs strong men to handle its business; to protect the women, children, and elders; and to help guide the young men into manhood.

To the women I tricked and manipulated with false promises of the so-called good life: I'm sorry. You had no idea that you were flirting with a potential life sentence from the Feds just by associating with me. Some of you were unintentionally caught up in my case and faced federal prosecution. Not only could you have lost your life in more ways than one, but you could have also lost your children to Child Protective Services—or even worse—watched them murdered by someone wanting to rob, kill, or kidnap me.

I apologize to the fathers to whom I sold crack. Many of you were at one time good, strong, vibrant men in the community who had good jobs. Before using drugs you had been decent husbands and fathers. You were schoolteachers, construction workers, and postal employees. Some of you lost it all because of the drugs.

Due to drug use, many fathers in the community were absent because they were too busy getting high. They were chasing highs as their babies went hungry and unattended while their fathers wildly ran around on crack missions.

My most sincere apology goes to my grandmother Gladys Starks—may she rest in peace. When I came home from prison, our reunion was moving and painful. She gave me a big bear hug and nearly suffocated me. Her eyes watering, she looked me square in the face and said, "Son, the years that you were gone took years off of my life and hurt me more than they hurt you." I stayed strong for that moment and didn't break down crying, but as soon as I got in my car and drove away, I wept like a baby. Those were the most painful words anyone has ever said to me.

This apology letter is not a sleight of hand to solicit empathy under the umbrella of being self-deprecating and insecure, wanting people to feel sorry for me; it is simply a genuine apology that I feel compelled to give. This letter is therapeutic and cleansing for me. It is a step toward healing and reconciliation for myself, the community, and maybe even you, the reader.

The Black community is in a state of emergency. The crack epidemic changed the course of history forever. And the carnage and wake of its destruction still affects us all deeply. Conceptually, its lingering effects compare to those of slavery; the overpowering effects of mass incarceration and the persistent, modern devastation of the Black family can easily be connected to the havoc wreaked by crack. I will forever feel spiritually tainted by taking part in this catastrophe.

As a community, Black folks are suffering at disproportionate levels when it comes to negative indicators like incarceration rates, new HIV infections, high school dropout stats, and so on. I believe these are all direct side effects of the crack-cocaine epidemic and its far-reaching ramifications. This epidemic is one of the latest manifestations of the plague that has been imposed upon the Black community, leading to its imminent destruction and dismantling. My community, though still here and still fighting, will never be the same.

In the spirit of atonement, I promise to continue to educate myself on many different levels and share that information with my community. Further, I promise to never again knowingly participate in any activity that will negatively impact my community.

One Love,
Malik

DO NOT PRAY FOR AN EASY LIFE,
PRAY FOR THE STRENGTH
TO ENDURE A HARD ONE.
—*Bruce Lee*

ACKNOWLEDGMENTS

To the God of my understanding, without you nothing would be possible.

To my parents, Patricia Sullivan and John Wade; my stepfather, Machon Sullivan; my wife, Jewell; my daughter, Alexis; my sisters, Shirelle, Mionka, and Shivon; and my brother, John, who have all loved and supported me unconditionally.

To my immediate family who always had positive words of motivation about this book project, my uncle Leroy Wise; my uncle and his wife, Myron and Sonja Bryant; aunt Cynthia Wise; cousins Rhonda and Carol Alexander, Rico, Maisha and Akeem, Leonard Doss, Johnny Malone, and Craig Moore; Aron, Angie, and Malika Wise; Saunders Mabrey; Quindena Dudley; Keith and Surre Smith; Andrew Gordon; Tracy Douglas; Delvon Anderson; and Eric Moore.

To my extended family who has always acknowledged and respected me and my vision, Maurice, Shelley, and Charles Tatum; James Beasley; Maiyio and Kim Mitchell.

To my Minnesota family, Samar, Daola, Sidney, Devon, and Betty Moseley.

To my friends who have supported me loyally, Jermaine Boddie, Zack Revell, Ed Donaldson, Kareim "BP" Malone, Asani Shakur, Willie Earl, Ray Kelley, Jason Johnson, Dr. Mark Robinson, Jerrell "Junebug" Benjamin, Carl Jacobs, Derek "Shooter" Williams, Patrick Cotton, Steve Bledsoe, Jesse Brown, and Sitka Simmons.

To my SIG family and all the young men I work with in the community.

To my co-defendants, Percy Dillon and Jerron Lollis, for being stand-up guys.

To my team, without you this book would not be possible: Pete Gort, Cathy Jackson, editors Dana Fitchett and Tammy Ditmore, project manager Marla Markman, social media guy John Murray, mentor and advisor Hal Shelton, photographer Jayvon "Hitz," videographer Jordan Ching, Jerome Palencia from Northbound Media, and Kendrick Anderson.

Special thanks to Dr. Julianne Malveaux and San Francisco Public Defender Jeff Adachi for supporting my project.

Thanks to Diane Grey from 100% College Prep and Rudy Corpuz from United Playaz.

Thanks to Herm Lewis, Sean "Stone" Ramsey, Clifford "Spud" Johnson, Bryson Clark from Royally Melanated Publishing, and Robert "Fleetwod" Bowden and Shawn Ginwright for their industry advice.

Made in the USA
Columbia, SC
01 August 2019